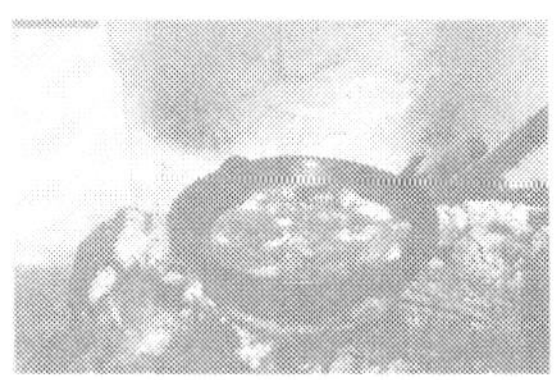

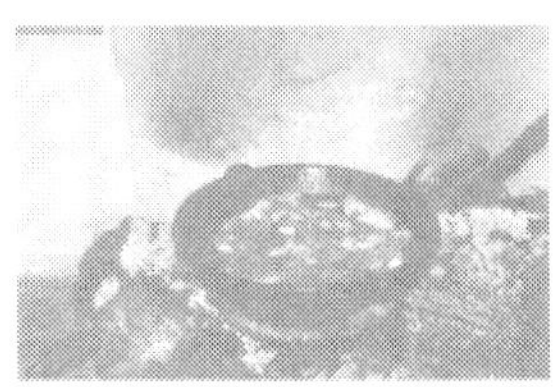

M. Margarida Pereira-Müller

MY AUNTS' RECIPES

The food of Cabeço de Vide

Titel: My aunts' recipes - The food of Cabeço de Vide

Author: M. Margarida Pereira-Müller

Email: guidapereiramuller@gmail.com

ISBN: 9798369736890

Independently published

To Joana, Daniela and Sebastian

To Oliver, Sofia and Marianna

Cabeço de Vide

There are few records regarding the foundation of the village of Cabeço-de-Vide. It has been occupied by humans since the Neolithic, perhaps because it has water throughout the year, thanks to the creeks of Vide and Vidigão. The Romans were here — the famous Roman road, a subsidiary road of the important Roman military road, that linked Mérida to Lisbon, served the Sulfúrea thermal springs, where ruins of a bathhouse and many other archaeological remains dating from Roman times have been found all over the place. Even today you can see the remains of the Roman road, made of large basalt slabs with well-delineated edges, on the dirt track that starts near the Sulfúrea park and goes up to the top of the village.

According to stories told around the fireplace, the name comes from the rugged life of its inhabitants. The first settlement was built next to the creek, but for reasons that have never been fully ascertained, people would fall ill and die. It was then decided to move to the top of the hill that rose right there. The death rate decreased and the inhabitants gave the village the name Cabeço da Vida, which became Cabeço de Vide. However, the town's coat of arms contains a vine and there are those who speak of a large vine that was here when the village was founded.

Another legend mentions a great battle that took place here. The many dead that were left unburied led to an outbreak of plague that killed many of the inhabitants. The survivors climbed the hill and recovered their health - the name of the place, Cabeço de Vide, the hill that gave life, was born.

Objectively, the story is different. In 1160, King Afonso Henriques conquered the land, which was retaken and destroyed by the Arabs in 1190. A few years later it was rebuilt on top of the hill to better defend itself from the enemies. A castle was then built or rebuilt, at an altitude of 340 m, and a walled enclosure was erected around the village, which was destroyed in 1710 by the Castilians. The battles for possession of the village went on and on. In 1211, King Afonso II transferred the knightly monks from Evora to Avis, giving them a huge fief, which included Cabeço de Vide, and entrusting them with the defence of the Upper Alentejo. Finally, in 1240, King Sancho II stormed the fortress of Vaiamonte and expelled the Saracens from the Upper Alentejo for good.

In 1512, Cabeço de Vide was awarded a charter by King Manuel I.

In the 16th century, Cabeço de Vide was donated to an

illustrious man-at-arms: Diogo de Azambuja. This was the golden age of the town which began, in 1498, with the foundation of the Santa Casa da Misericórdia by Queen D. Leonor. The main building, which is next to the parish church, includes the 15th century hospital, the 16th century church with its marble altar and the brotherhood's Mesary Room. The decline of the town began during the Restoration campaigns.

Several noblemen held positions in the Town Hall of Cabeço de Vide, among them some members of the Vaz de Camões family, who lived in the Avis Street. According to information from the Junta de Freguesia, "their descendants remained here for over two centuries". It is known that they belonged to the lower nobility and "that they owned an estate, still called "Monte de Camões". It was on this estate that my grandmother Marianna was born in 1883, as we can read in the baptism register, which is in the District Archive of Portalegre.

The best view over the new part of the town and the whole region is undoubtedly from the top. The ideal location is the small Largo da Cadeia (the Prison's Square), where the pillory, a hexagonal granite column on three steps, stands.

To the left there is a small house which was once the town hall. Cabeço de Vide was a municipality until 1855, when it became part of Alter do Chão Municipality.

On the right side is the old prison with a square-shaped Clock Tower. On the marble clock "dial" you can still read the date of the building's construction: 1570. The present clock was given in 1951 by Joaquim Firmino Costa Pinto and Beatriz Fernandes Vaz on their Silver Anniversary.

Next to what remains of the castle is the 16th century mannerist-style parish church, where I was baptised on December 26, 1957. This is where the image of Nossa Senhora das Candeias (Our Lady of Light), the village's patron, is kept.

Like most Alentejan villages and towns, Cabeço de Vide has its houses whitewashed, with windows and doors painted either blue (to ward off evil spirits) or bright yellow.

Besides the Sulfúrea bath, what stands out in the village is its huge *Rossio* (main square), the largest in Portugal. It is a wide avenue, 600 metres long, officially called Avenida da Libertação (Liberation Avenue) since 1932, when the town ceased to belong to the municipality of Alter do Chão and became part of the municipality of Fronteira. At one end of the Rossio is the primary school and, at the other end, an 18th century manor house, the Solar Simões Cardoso. King D. Carlos I stayed here overnight in November 1907.

Close to the manor house, stands the 16th century Church of the Holy Spirit. The roof is concealed by a series of truncated parallelepiped battlements; the bell tower is classical, with a 16th century bell, another 17th century bell, and a bell in the upper eye. The main door of the church leads to the Largo do Espírito Santo, where a marble cross stands.

Espírito Santo chruch and the marble cross

The centre of Rossio is a wide promenade, flanked by orange and mulberry trees along its length, with small fishponds, waterfalls, and fountains to quench the thirst of those who stroll along. It invites you to enjoy long and pleasant talks, especially at the end of the day when, in the summer, the heat decreases.

There are many churches in Cabeço de Vide, but I will mention only two. The Church of Nossa Senhora dos Anjos, at the top of the street with the same name (formerly Rua do Forno), is the home of the image of the Virgin, which the villagers dress in light blue in times of drought.

In the lower part of the village, there is the Calvary Church, circular, like most Calvary churches.

There are two other famous places in the village. One is the railway station, now deactivated, and the Sulfúrea thermal springs.

The old railway station keeps some of the beautiful polychrome tile panels, painted by Leopoldo Batistini, in 1933, with Alentejo scenes: pigs in the fields, olive picking, horse breeding, sheep herding, wheat threshing, cork stripping, ploughing with mules, the sowing, the harvest, the transport of wheat for threshing, country costumes. At the top of the façade, there is a flower-framed panel, with the coat of arms in the centre.

Cabeço de Vide railway station

The thermal baths are not far from the railway station. The gardens around the thermal house, with their large old trees, make Sulfúrea an oasis in summer. The Junta de Freguesia (parish council) built a natural pool in the creek that runs through the gardens, retaining the waters through sluices.

Súlfurea natural swimming pool

The medicinal waters come from four springs and contain sulphuric acid. Hence the name Sulfúrea. The water is recommended for various diseases, mainly respiratory, skin, rheumatic and musculoskeletal.

Thermal waters were already known 3.500 years ago. It was the Romans who first used them for therapeutic purposes and built a thermal bath.

The first thermal baths of the modern era were built in 1855 by local people. At that time, besides being used for local therapeutics, the water was bottled and sold all over the country, having even been distinguished with silver medals in two International Exhibitions: in the second half of the 20th century in Paris and in 1922 in Rio de Janeiro.

On the way out of the village, to Fronteira, a gallow can still be seen in the middle of the fields. This is the only known example in Portugal that escaped destruction following the abolition of the death penalty - as we know, Cabeço de Vide ceased to be the county seat in 1855, this fact may have motivated the non-destruction of this monument. With the move, people forgot to destroy the gallow.

Death by hanging was very common in ancient historical periods - for example, in Rome, the gallows were for Roman citizens, as barbarians (non-Roman, foreigners) were crucified. Portugal was the second country in Europe, after the Grand Duchy of Tuscany (1786), to abolish the death penalty. In 1852, it was abolished for political crimes by Queen Maria II. In the following decade, in 1867, it was abolished for civil crimes, except for treason during the war.

The gallow consists of two masonry parallelepiped obelisks. It complemented the pillory in cases of death penalty, and, unlike the latter, it was always located outside the town. The condemned was hung by a rope around his neck, suspended from a horizontally crossed beam and supported by the prisms which are still in place today.

The gallow

Who were the condemned on this gallow? Certainly, serious criminals. But who knows if Jews persecuted by the Inquisition might not have died there? We know by reading the reports of the Inquisition of Évora that, in Cabeço de Vide, there was a large and active Jewish community in the 16th and 17th centuries. In fact, Cabeço de Vide would have been, at that time, one of the Alentejo's villages most affected by the Inquisition's terror: between 1533-1668, 211 *videnses* would have been condemned by penalties ranging from abjuration, loss of goods, prison, torture, having turned this village into one of the most sacrificed by the strong arm of the Inquisition of Évora.

My aunts

When Aunt Maria, my eldest aunt, died, the family gathered in the old family house to share the family belongings. In the bottom of a chest of clothes, we found a military service booklet. I asked, surprised, why my aunts had kept the military book of a João Alves Coelho... Aunt Olga, Uncle Heitor's wife, replied even more surprised: "So, Guidinha, don't you know?! It was your grandfather!" I answered: "What do you mean with *my grandfather*? His name was Alves Pereira, just like my father, José Alves Pereira, and me." She then explained that our grandfather was a republican and, to escape the Monarchist Guard, he had left Castanheira de Pera, where he was born, come to the Alentejo and changed his name to João Alves Pereira.

My curiosity was piqued. I began to investigate. The story could even be right... In the District Archive of Leiria I found a baptism certificate: "On the twenty fifth of July of the year one thousand eight hundred and eighty one, in this parish church of São Domingos da Castanheira, council of Pedrogam Grande, diocese of Coimbra, I solemnly baptized a male individual, whom I named João, born in Carregal Fundeiro, in this parish, at seven o'clock in the afternoon, legitimate son of Luíz Alves Coelho and Maria da Conceição, workers, born in Sarzedas de São Pedro, where they live, parishioners and neighbours, paternal grandson of Miguel Alves Coelho and Anna Dinis, maternal grandson of João Domingues Novo (?) and Joaquina Maria. Godfathers (...) And for the record I have drawn up in duplicate this document which has been read and checked by the godfathers who did not sign because they do not know how to write, Era ut supra. The Rector Manuel Joaquim Rodrigues Correia".

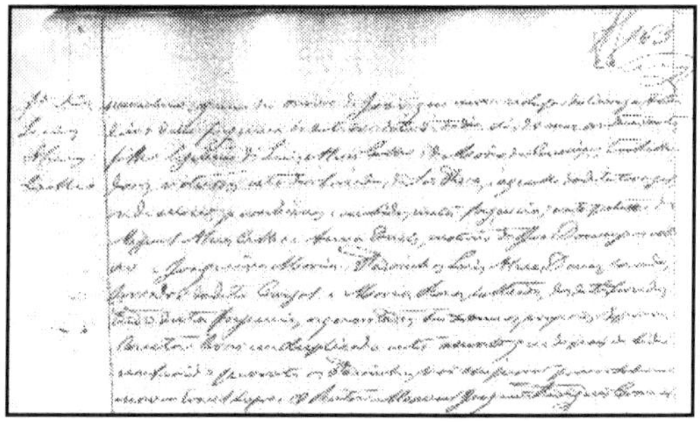

Baptism record of João Alves Coelho

Now, the names of the paternal grandparents that appear on the baptism certificates of João Alves Pereira's children match with the names of his parents!

When my grandfather left Castanheira de Pera and went to the Alentejo is not known. There is no military service record of a João Alves Coelho in the Military Archives - although I have seen the military service booklet, which has since disappeared.

Where did he choose to live? When did he change his

name from Coelho to Pereira? We don't know.
He might have started his Alentejan adventure in Alagoa, near Portalegre, since he was known in Cabeço de Vide as "O Alagoa" (and his aunts as "The Alagoa girls").
He was a travelling salesman and used to go around that part of the Alto Alentejo in a cart, selling textiles and garns—in short, haberdashery. And possibly on one of these trips to Cabeço de Vide he met Marianna who "On the 20th day of January of one thousand eight hundred eighty four, in this parish church of Cabeço de Vide, parish of Nossa Senhora das Candeias, Alter do Chão Council, Diocese of Portalegre, I, the priest João Neves da Silva, Prior of this same parish, solemnly baptised and anointed with the Holy Oils a female child whom I named Marianna, born in this parish at three o'clock on the evening of the second day of November of last year, the legitimate/ first name/ daughter of Francisco José Sardinheiro, farmer, born in this town, and Cecília da Conceição* from Vaiamonte, County of Monforte, Archbishopric of Évora, ... parishioners of this parish and residents of Monte de Camões estate, paternal granddaughter of Joaquim José Sardinheiro and Francisca Maria,

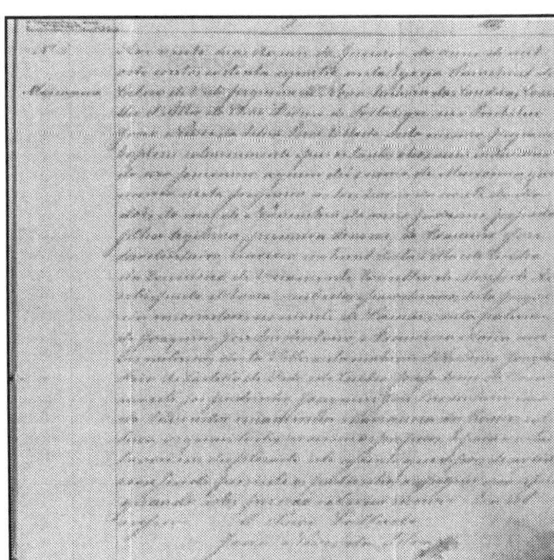

Marianna's baptism record

both natives of this town, maternal granddaughter of António Joaquim Feio de Castello de Vide and Cecília

Josefa Pereira de Vaiamonte(?)".
They must have been married between 1910 and 1912. The records for these years have disappeared. They are neither in the District Archive of Portalegre, nor in the Alter do Chão Conservatory, nor in the Parish Archive of Cabeço de Vide. The monarchy was overthrown on October 5th, 1910 and was replaced by a Republican political system. Chaotic years followed. Many records were lost.
I also don't know when they started living in the house at Rua de Avis 30-32. What is certain is that it was here that the four children were born, because fortunately the birth registers exist. The eldest daughter, Maria Cecília Pereira, was born on April 7th, 1913. In her birth certificate, we can read that she is the daughter of João Alves Pereira, her paternal grandfather is Luíz Alves (neither Coelho nor Pereira) and her paternal grandmother is Maria da Conceição Pereira (a surname she never had).

Rua de Avis

When registering their 2nd child, Heitor Alves Pereira, the names of the paternal grandparents were the same, but when registering their 3rd child, Cecília dos Ramos Pereira, the real name of her paternal grandfather, Luíz Alves Coelho, was given. For the 4th child, my father, José Alves Pereira, the paternal grandfather's name becomes Luíz Alves Pereira again, but his grandmother loses the surname Pereira, remaining only Maria da Conceição.
On the ground floor of the house, with the door number 30, my grandfather opened a fabric and haberdashery

shop - in other words, he continued to do what he used to do before he got married, only not as a travelling salesman, but in a "real" shop.
It seems that life was going well. My grandfather was also a farmer, with some estates in Cabeço de Vide: Monte Camões, where grandmother Marianna was born, another estate in Passo Miúdo and six parts of another estate in Azinhaga das Vinhas.

All of a sudden, Marianna died from peritonitis, aged 38, on February 21st, 1925, "at the house of her residence, without leaving a will or any last will disposition, leaving the following heirs:
- Children -

1° Maria Cecília Pereira, minor, 11 years old,

2° Heitor Alves Pereira, minor, nine years old,

3° Cecília dos Ramos Pereira, minor, six years old,

4° José Alves Pereira, minor, four years old,

all living with the declarant in Cabeço de Vide".

Thus, from one moment to the next, the life of this family took a great turn. What was it like, in the first quarter of the 20th century, for a man to have four under-age children without the support of a woman? Of course, the women of the family must have stepped in to help with the so-called "women's tasks". The eldest daughter, Aunt Maria, must have been given the task of looking after the house and her siblings. At the age of 11, she should already know how to do almost all house chores.

Some years later João married Maria Filipina Costa, a widow who lived in Assumar. She was a lady with a very distinctive bearing. Being married to a cloth merchant, she refused to mend sheets and towels. She would have died in the early 1960s. One of my earliest memories is of her. I must have been about three years old. I liked Granny very much (for me she was our Granny). The house has a dangerous step at the top of the stairs and the women of the house were always warning us, girls, to be careful. She could see very badly, despite wearing glasses with very thick lenses and black frames. And I remember taking her hand and telling her that I would help her down the step. Childish innocence!

One of the times we went back to Cabeço de Vide, Granny was no longer there. Only Grandpa and the aunts. Grandfather loved me very much. I loved playing in the shop. Opening the drawer where he kept the money to listen to the little bell at the bottom - he explained that this was how he would listen if, by chance, someone wanted to steal the money from the till.

I liked to sit on the counter of the shop - something that was forbidden because, as Grandfather used to say, it would bring bad luck. I knew that, and yet I sat there anyway, so that he could take me off and sit me on his lap, where I could play with the gold watch chain that he wore attached to his waistcoat.

My Aunts never married. It seems that there were suitors, but Grandfather didn't want them to marry. Maybe to have someone to look after him? Who knows?

Aunt Maria, a small, introverted woman, was the owner of the kitchen and spent the day around the fireplace, the pots, and pans (there had to be pots with water around the fireplace to always have hot water available). She was the one who always cooked. As soon as she woke up, she would rekindle the fire and start cooking lunch. After lunch, she would do the dishes and start preparing dinner.

My aunt Maria preparing the fire place (1983)

Aunt Cecília, an extroverted and talkative woman, was the confectioner and the one who took over the shop when Grandfather died in 1969.

There was no running water in Cabeço de Vide until after the 25th of April Revolution. When the watercarrier arrived, it was a whirlwind in that house with all the women carrying the pitchers up and down the stairs. Between the watercarriers' visits, the women would go with a pitcher on their heads, with or without a wheel, to fetch water from the fountain. As I always wanted to go to the fountain with them, they made me a *rodilha* (a piece of cloth that is folded lengthwise many times until it forms a thick strip of fabric that is coiled up around itself like a tight spiral, then placed on the top of the head, just like a crown) and gave me a small pitcher, but I was afraid of breaking it and I always carried it side-ways, on my waist.

Childhood memories include our trips to Camões estate with Grandfather. We would go in the cart pulled by the mare. Beside us, the dog would run, which always had the name of a river. I remember the Tagus and then the Douro. Aunt Cecília always went on foot too, because... she got sick. I never understood how one could get sick riding a cart, but she got sick in any means of transport - even in the cart!

My father by the rabbit hutch (1983)

The animals - chickens, rabbits, ducks, pigs - were looked after by the two aunts. The pigs ate our leftovers, so there was very little garbage. Every day, the two aunts would take a bucket of water and creolin and scrubbed the two white pigs they had in the family hog pen in the courtyard. In fact, that pigsty was always very clean. Those pigs were not pigs at all. At Camões estate the situation was different. The pigs were black and dirty and the hog pen ... was really a pigsty.

When the whole family gathered in Cabeço de Vide, the

meals were long. We all sat around the big round table in the leaving room. Grandfather had his rightful place, under the wall clock, in front of the door. It was the patriarch's seat; when Grandpa died, that seat was taken by Uncle Heitor, his eldest son. The swinging of the clock's pendulum, which struck the hours at the full hour, was loud and could be very clearly heard. In the drawing-room, which was at the other end of the house, there was another clock, the noise of whose pendulum echoed through the living-room and the bedrooms.

The table had a hole in the middle, at the bottom, where, in winter, the aunts would put hot coal. A long tablecloth (*camilha)* covered the whole table up to the floor and I remember pulling it over my lap to feel the heat and enjoy that special smell of the embers. Embers radiate a more consistent form of heat, as opposed to an open fire, which is constantly changing along with the heat it radiates

On one wall of the room there were a series of paintings that fascinated me. One of them was a set of two paintings: one represented a friendly couple and the other an angry couple. There was also a picture frame made of cork, in filigree work, and another silk filigree frame with the picture of my older sister as a baby - the first granddaughter of Grandma and Grandpa. We kept those frames which were returned to their original place when we renovated the house to remind us of who passed through the house.

Aunt Maria cooked very well and everything she made was very tasty. They were strong foods, very slow cooked. In the winter, she cooked by the fireplace and, in the summer, in the wood cooker. The cakes and biscuits, made by Aunt Cecília, were baked in the wood cooker oven. Later, my Mother gave the aunts a cloche, a portable, electric oven.

Another occasion of frenetic activity was the hog slaughter. There were some men in the village who were experts. Grandfather, and later Uncle Heitor, would set the day and inform my father by letter - we were amused by the letter, which invariably said "the very sharp knives are ready". We immediately imagined countless thrillers...

On the day of the slaughter there was a lot of coming and going at home. In the courtyard a wooden slight incline stall was set up, temporary, where the men would lay down the hog after having been tied up. With a precision, the person in charge of the slaughter would stab a very long, and very sharp knife into the neck of the pig, hitting it directly in the superior vena cava (carotid artery). If done correctly, blood should exit the body rapidly . (I remember with horror the pig's squeals. One year, the pig broke free and, with the knife already stuck in it, overturned the stall, and started running around the yard. A traumatic scene).

Meanwhile, my aunts had already prepared a clay bowl

with vinegar to get the blood that drained from the animal and that had to be constantly stirred. With this blood, they would later make the *cachola* soup with lots of cumin. The blood that was not stirred was boiled in pieces and then seasoned.

After the animal was killed, the men prepared a fire and with brooms made of wild branches they passed these brooms over the pig, scorching its hair. Then the pig was scraped and washed with water and salt. Finally, the men tore the skin that preceded the tendons of the hind legs and hung the carcass with a thick rope from the *chambaril*, an arched piece of wood, in the middle of the court, on the main beam. Again, the aunts would place bowls on the ground to receive the rest of the animal's blood and offal that would fall out once the pig was opened.

The men would then cut the pig from top to bottom. The giblets were carefully removed and washed with vinegar. The guts were washed in water and then rubbed with a mixture of vinegar, lemon, orange, and salt to remove their unpleasant smell. The *bucho* (stomach) was poured out and very well washed. The bladder was given to the children to make a ball out of it.

Once the evisceration was finished, the pig was washed inside, covered with a white cloth, and left to cool until the following day.

In the meantime, some women would begin to prepare the delicacies of the slaughter day: *sopa da cachola* and the cheeks, the steaks, the kidney, and the heart, seasoned with coarse salt and roasted over an open fire.

The next day, the pig was then cut up. Each type of meat would be put in a different bowl, as it had several uses. This work was done exclusively by women, who prepared the meat and the fat for the different types of sausages and for preservation.

Railway map

When my sister Lena and I started going by ourselves to Cabeço de Vide, by train, during the summer holidays, our mother always sent a telegram to the aunts, telling them what time the train was expected to arrive. It was a long journey: from Santa Apolónia, in Lisbon, to Portalegre on an electrified line, the so-called Eastern Line, created in 1863 to connect Lisbon to Elvas (later it only connected Abrantes to Elvas). "Don't forget", our mother reminded us of before we left, "after Chança, Mata, Crato, it's Portalegre, and you have to get off the train and catch the motor car". This one had only wooden seats, not very comfortable. As the journey was short, it didn't matter. At the beginning of 1990, the Portalegre Branch Line, which had been inaugurated on 21st January 1949 and connected the Estremoz station to the East Line, was closed and transformed into a cycle track, the "Ecopista dos Atoleiros", which today links Fronteira to Cabeço de Vide.

Often, the telegram would arrive later than we did. So, our aunts weren't waiting for us at the train station, and the two of us would go up the Roman road to surprise them. Whether they knew we were coming or whether it was a surprise, we always gave them great joy. They were happy to have us there. They spoiled us from the first moment to the last, with the foods we liked best - even buying Spanish chocolate bars from the smuggler, which, by the way, we didn't like... But it was worth the effort. Those were happy days. In their loving memory, I wrote this book.

The three nieces by the gate (1961?)

The three nieces eating grapes in the small estate (1970)

Starters

Açorda (Bread soup)

Açorda is an Arab legacy. It was considered a poor man's food as it consists only of bread, garlic, herbs (coriander or pennyroyal) and water, seasoned with a dash of olive oil and salt. Some people replace the water with codfish stock, and if so, add some cooked codfish shreds.

1 bunch of coriander (or pennyroyal, or if you prefer, a mixture of coriander and pennyroyal)
3 cloves of garlic, peeled
1 tablespoon coarse salt
4 tablespoons olive oil
1.5 l water
4 eggs

400 g stale bread, sliced or diced

In a mortar, crush herbs, garlic, and coarse salt with a pestle until it mushy.
Boil water and poach eggs in it.
Place the mixture of herbs and garlic in the tureen, drizzle with olive oil and pour the boiling water in which you poached the eggs.
Place bread in the tureen and the poached eggs on top (you can serve the poached eggs on the side if you wish).

Cabeça de carneiro assada (Roast lamb's head)

Normally this dish is made with many lamb or mutton heads. If you buy them at the butcher's, the heads come already washed and without their nostrils. If you slaughter your self the animals, you will have to wash them and remove the nostrils.

Lamb or mutton heads
3 cloves of garlic per head, peeled
Coarse salt
Pepper
Vinegar

Lard

Heat the oven to 225 °C.
In a mortar, crush garlic with salt and rub the heads with this paste. Place them in a roasting pan, preferably a clay one. Season with pepper. Spread lard all over and, finally, drizzle with vinegar.
Roast in the oven. From time to time, turn over and pour the sauce that will form over them.
The roasted heads can be eaten hot or cold.

Canja de galinha (Chicken soup)

Aunt Maria's chicken soup was wonderful. It wasn't surprising because it was made with one of the chickens that roamed the courtyard of the house plucking what they found on the ground. I loved to pick the letter pasta and play with my sisters, trying to form words before eating them. The meat was usually used for other dishes or pies.

.

Playing with chicks (1972)

1 chicken
1 onion, peeled
4 cloves
Salt

Per person,
1 tablespoon letter pasta

Boil chicken in a large pan with cold water, salt and an onion studded with cloves. When it comes to the boil, lower the heat and cook until the chicken meat starts to come off the bones.
Strain the broth and return to the heat. When it boils, add the pasta and let it cook.

Canja de peru (Turkey soup)

For Christmas Day lunch, the turkey soup, made with the turkey kids, neck and feet, was a must.

Turkey giblets
Turkey feet
Turkey neck
1 onion
1 bay leaf
Salt
1 cup of rice
Sprig of mint (optional)

Grabbing a turkey (1964)

Bring a pan to the boil with giblets, legs, neck, onion, bay leaf, salt and 1 ½ l cold water and cook for 45 minutes.
Strain broth and debone legs, feet and neck. Slice the liver and giblets.

Bring stock back to the boil. Add rice and cook for 15 to 20 minutes.
Add the deboned meat and the sliced liver and giblets, and serve immediately. If you wish, you can add a sprig of mint.

Cabeça de xara (Cooked pork's head)

The "cabeça de xara" is a "cheese" (hence also known as "head cheese") made from the soft parts of the pork's head, seasoned with spices, herbs, white wine and vinegar. The preparation is long (4 days). The origin of this dish is unknown for sure. What er know that it is one of the oldest recorded recipes. It is mentioned in the book "The Modern Cook or the New Art of Cooking" by Lucas Rigaud, one of the chefs under D. Maria I and D. Pedro III, in 1788. and Pedro III, in 1788, as "Queijo de cabeça de porco" (Pork's head).

1 pork's head
Coarse salt
3 onions, peeled and roughly chopped
4 cloves garlic, peeled
6 peppercorns
1 tablespoon coriander seeds
1 tablespoon of cumin seeds
3 bay leaves
5 cloves

1 small bunch sage
1 small bunch marjoram
0.5 dl vinegar
3.5 dl white wine

Remove brains from head. Season head with plenty of coarse salt and leave for 48 hours.
After this time, wash head very well to remove excess salt, cut it into pieces and place it in a pan with the rest of the ingredients. Cover head with cold water.
Bring to the boil and cook until meat comes off the bones.
Debone and cut meat into small cubes.
Strain broth and put it back in the pan. Put meat back into the broth.
Put it back on the heat and let it boil for a few minutes.
Remove from the heat and drain.
Place meat inside a large cotton cloth and close it up, pinching the ends with thread or a strong tape.
Place on a board and put a weight on top (to ensure no air bubbles are trapped in the meat), and refrigerate until solidified, for 12 hours.
Cut into very thin slices and serve at room temperature.

Gaspacho à alentejana (Cold soup)

On hot summer days, my aunts used to make a delicious and fresh gazpacho. I remember well seeing aunt Cecília (this soup was always prepared by aunt Cecília, and not by aunt Maria) cutting tomato, cucumber and bell pepper in a bowl and then pouring cold water over the vegetbales.

3 garlic cloves
2 teaspoons coarse salt
2 tablespoons olive oil
2 tablespoons vinegar
Oregano
2 tomatoes, peeled and cut into small cubes
1 cucumber, peeled and cut into small cubes
1 green bell pepper, cut into small cubes
1.5 l ice-cold water
200 g stale bread, cut into small cubes

In a mortar, crush garlic and coarse salt with a pestle until it mushy.
Place in the tureen and drizzle with olive oil, vinegar and oregano. Stir well.
Add tomatoes, cucumber and bell pepper. Pour in cold water.
Add bread and serve chilled. Serve with fresh goat's cheese and slices of chorizo.

Labaças com feijão (Sorrel soup)

Some time ago I picked up some leaves on the field that I didn't quite know what they were. I asked my neighbour if she knew and if it would be OK to eat them: "This is sorrel! We used to eat this very often as a child, whenever we went to the fields. My mother used to make it all the time together with beans, but now I haven't eaten it for years." To make this very healthy dish, you have to go for a walk in the countryside in the spring and look for sorrel.

A bunch of sorrel
Olive oil
1 onion, peeled and chopped
Paprika
Coarse salt
1 or 2 bay leaves
Cooked beans

Wash sorrel and cut in smaller pieces with your hands. Bring a pan of water to the boil. When water boils, add sorrel and cook for 5 to 10 minutes. Drain and discard water. This step is important to remove the acidity and bitterness of the sorrel.
Heat olive oil in a pan and sauté onion with paprika, salt, and bay leaf. Add blanched sorrel and beans. Stir everything well. Add enough water for the soup, cover the pan, lower the heat and simmer for 10 minutes.

Miolos e rins com ovos mexidos (Brain and kidney with eggs)

Brains are one of those dishes that you are either love or hate. I am one of those who love eating brains, and I make this recipe only with the brains - without the kidneys.

2 lamb brains
Salt
4 lamb kidneys, cut into small pieces
Lard
1 onion, peeled and finely chopped
6 eggs, beaten
1 small piece of stale bread, crumbled

Poach brains in boiling water and salt.
Fry kidneys in lard. Add chopped onion.
Mix eggs with bread crumbles and add to the kidneys, as well as the poached brains.

Pezinhos de coentrada (Pig's trotters)

Cooked pig's trotters with coriander are one of the best known Alentejo delicacies. Ask the butcher to get the feet and cut them in half. The coriander is very important in this dish.

8 pig's trotters, cleaned and cut in half
Coarse salt
100 g lard
2 bunches of coriander, chopped
2 bay leaves
8 garlic cloves, peeled
3 tablespoons of flour
1 dl vinegar

Rub pig's trotters with salt and leave to rest for three days. After this time, rinse them in cold water to remove excess salt.
Bring to the boil in a pan and cook well. Remove from the pan and strain the stock through a fine-mesh strainer.
In a mortar, crush coriander with garlic and salt with a pestle.
Melt lard in a pan. Add the garlic and coriander paste and bay leaf.
Add the cooked pig's trotters and pour a little of the broth over them. Let it simmer for a while. Add flour mixed with vinegar. Lower the heat, and cook, stirring for 2 to 3 minutes more.
Serve with fried bread.

Sarapatel (Pork offal stew)

Sarapatel is a fiery, tangy dish that uses pork (or lamb) offal and blood and is eaten on the day the pigs are slaughtered. Vinegar is another important component. Served with slices of orange, it is less tangy.

1 kg pork blood
Pork heart/kidney/tongue (any offal of your choice or all), cut into small chunks
1 tablespoon lard
2 onions, peeled and chopped
2 tomatoes, diced
2 carrots, peeled and diced
250 g green beans, cut
1 bunch parsley, chopped
1 tablespoon vinegar
Salt
Sliced stale bread

Cook blood in boiling water. Combine pork, liver, and other offal in a large saucepan. Cover with water. Add salt. Cover and bring to a boil over medium-high heat. Stir once, reduce to a simmer, cover, and cook for 30 minutes. Skim liquid. Strain, reserving meat and broth separately.
Sauté onion, tomato, carrots, green beans and parsley in lard. Add offal broth. When it boils, lower the heat and cook, stirring for 2 to 3 minutes more.
Crumble the blood and add it to the soup. Sprinkle with

vinegar and stir the mixture. Bring to a simmer, cover, and cook for 30 minutes, stirring constantly with a wooden spoon until it is very juicy and relatively dry. Season to taste with salt.
Place the slices of bread in the bottom of the serving dish and pour in the soup.

Sopa de cachola (Offal soup)

For the soup we use the pork blood from the day of the slaughter and the offal.

Pork heart/kidney/tongue (any offal of your choice or all), cut into small chunks
2 dl olive oil
4 garlic cloves, peeled and chopped
2 onions, peeled and chopped
1 green bell pepper, diced
4 tomatoes, diced
2 bay leaves
Coarse salt
Parsley
Vinegar
Cumin
2.5 dl pork blood
Stale bread, sliced

Heat olive oil in a pan and sauté onions and garlic. Add pepper, tomato, bay leaf and parsley. Add cumin, offal, and pork blood. Add water. When it boils, lower the heat and simmer for a few minutes. Adjust the seasoning.

Place the slices of bread in a tureen and pour the soup over them. Serve with slices of orange.

Sopa de beldroegas (Purslane soup)

Purslane is a very old, spontaneous plant which is often considered a weed. It is rich in salicylic acid and has anti-inflammatory, depurative, and diuretic properties.

2 bunches of purslane
1 dl olive oil
3 garlic cloves, peeled and chopped
500 g potatoes, peeled and diced
1 tablespoon paprika
Salt

Clean purslane and bring it to the boil in a pan with water. After a few minutes, drain and rinse under cold water.
Put olive oil, garlic, potatoes, and paprika in a pan and sauté everything well.
Add purslane and enough water for the soup. Boil until everything is cooked.
Serve very hot. If you want, you can poach some eggs in the soup.

Sopa de cação (Shark soup)

This sandbar shark soup might come from the Arabic moray eel soup, which is also eaten with bread. In former times this soup was eaten almost exclusively by the lower classes, as the price of sandbar shark was low, possibly due to the difficulty in preparing it and removing its typical smell and flavour. Hence the use of aromatic herbs.

4 large cuts of sandbar shark
2 dl olive oil
4 garlic cloves, peeled and finely chopped
1 bunch coriander, chopped
1 bay leaf
2 tablespoons flour
2 teaspoons paprika
2 tablespoons vinegar
1 tablespoon of flour
Salt and pepper
Stale bread, thinly sliced

Clean sandbar shark and soak in water, vinegar, salt and bay leaf for 1 - 2 hours.
Heat the olive oil and sauté garlic and coriander. Add 1 litre of water (the amount needed for the soup) and add the soaked sandbar shark.
When it comes to the boil, lower the heat and simmer until the sandbar shark is cooked.
In a bowl, dissolve flour and paprika in vinegar and 2 dl cold water. Add this mixture to the soup and cook for a

few minutes, gently shaking the pan. Taste to season. Place bread in the bottom of a tureen. Pour in the soup. Place the sandbar shark on top. Serve immediately.

Sopa de feijão frade (Kidney bean soup)

Kidney beans are rich in protein and fibre as well.

500 dl kidney beans, soaked overnight
1 dl olive oil
4 garlic cloves, peeled and chopped
1 onion, peeled and chopped
1 red bell pepper, diced
2 -3 ripe tomatoes, diced
Coarse salt
4 eggs
1 handful of chopped coriander
Sliced Alentejo bread, toasted

Drain beans, transfer to a pot. Cover with water and bring to a boil. Cook over low heat for 2-3h or until the beans are cooked.

In a pan, sauté garlic and onion in hot olive oil. Add bell pepper and tomato and let it simmer. Season with salt. Add kidney beans with broth and mix well. Let it simmer for a few minutes.

Poach eggs in the soup.

Place the bread in a tureen. Pour the soup over the bread, and garnish with the coriander.

Sopa de feijão redondo

(Round beans soup)

This recipe was given to me by Ana Luísa, who has a stall in the market in Portalegre and explains to her customers what to do with the vegetables she sells.

500 dl round dry beans, soaked overnight
1 dl olive oil
2 - 3 potatoes, peeled and diced
1 carrot, peeled and diced
1 turnip, peeled and diced
Coarse salt
Portuguese cabbage, shredded

Drain beans, transfer them to a pot. Cover with water and bring to a boil. Cook over low heat for 2-3h or until beans are cooked. Set aside.

Cook potatoes, carrot, and turnip in a pan. Season with salt.

Add beans and broth and mix everything well. Let simmer for a few minutes.

Add the shredded cabbage and let it cook. Serve.

Sopa de grão com nabiças

(Chickpea soup with turnip greens)

Chickpeas are a very important legume in our diet and should be consumed much more often than we do. It is a good source of protein, fibre, minerals such as iron, calcium, magnesium, phosphorus, potassium and B vitamins.

150 g dry chickpeas, soaked overnight
Coarse salt
1 bunch fresh (or frozen) spinach
4 tablespoons olive oil
1 onion, peeled and chopped
4 cloves garlic, peeled and chopped
1 bunch coriander
4 tablespoon elbows or other short pasta

Soak chickpeas in plenty of cold water overnight.
The next day, drain chickpeas. Put in the pan, add plenty cold water, season with salt and cook for 45 minutes (or 25 minutes if using the pressure cooker).
If using fresh spinach, pick the spinach, wash it and leave it to drain.
Heat olive oil in a large pan and sauté onion, garlic and coriander. Add spinach and cook for a little longer.
Add chickpeas with the broth. When it boils, add the pasta and cook for 6-7 minutes.
Taste and adjust seasoning and serve immediately.

Sopa de tomate (Tomato soup)

In the summer, I used to eat the tomato soup my aunts made with fleshy and very tasty tomatoes that they had in the small estate near Sulfúrea and in the Camões estate. To make this soup, my aunts peeled the tomato and removed the seeds. I don't remove anything. I use the whole tomato.

2 tablespoons olive oil
2 onions, peeled and sliced
5 garlic cloves, peeled and chopped
1 kg ripe tomatoes, cut into small pieces
2 bay leaves
Oregano and/or pennyroyal
Salt
4 eggs
Stale bread, sliced

Sauté garlic and onion in hot olive oil. When onions are translucent, add tomato, bay leaf, oregano (and/or pennyroyal) and season with salt.
Add a little water. When it boils, poach eggs in the soup.
Place bread in the bottom of a tureen. Pour the soup over the bread and serve.

Túberas com ovos (Mushorooms with eggs)

The "atúberas", as they say in Alentejo, are mushrooms of the truffle family. You can make "migas", rice or eat them with scrambled eggs.

1 kg *túberas*
Coarse salt
6 eggs, beaten
1 bunch parsley, finely chopped
1 small onion, peeled and finely chopped
Olive oil

Wash *túberas* very well and skin them. Wash them again and again and make sure you have removed all the soil. Slice them and season them with salt.
Heat olive oil in a frying pan and fry *túberas* in batches. Remove and keep warm.
In the same pan, lightly fry the onions. Add eggs and parsley. Finally, put *túberas* back in the pan and pour the eggs on top and let them stock.
This dish can be served as a side dish or as a snack.

Sausages

Cacholeira

The cacholeira *is the only sausage made with wine. As we can read in the book "Os enchidos de Cabeço de Vide", published by João Ribeirinho Leal, "for* cacholeiras *we use the meat from the pork head, the pancreas, and the liver".*

Pork shoulder with a little bit of fat, diced into smallish 1 -inch (2.5-cm) cubes
Paprika powder
Garlic, peeled and chopped
Coarse salt

Cloves

Pork liver
White wine

Pork casings

Pound chopped garlic in a mortar and pestle with a pinch of salt. If you don't have a pestle and mortar, crush the garlic and salt on your board using the flat of your knife.

Season pork with the garlic paste, paprika and cloves.

Crush liver, beating it with a knife until it crumbles. Add seasoned pork and wine.

Fill the casings with the meat-liver mixture. Tie off one end of the sausage with a thin string, making a simple knot. Tie the other end and swing the sausage like a jump rope. Make another simple knot.

Cook in a pan with water. Always keep the water at the same temperature to prevent the casings from bursting.

Once cooked, hang them on a rod and smoke them for a few days.

They can be eaten boiled or roasted.

Chouriço de carne (Cured meat *chouriço*)

The sausages were created from the need to preserve and use meat stained with blood and meat with some nerves. What the rest of the country calls "chouriço", we call "linguiça" in the Alentejo.

1.3 kg pork leg, diced into smallish 1-inch (2.5-cm) cubes
400 g pork belly, diced into smallish 1-inch (2.5-cm) cubes
200 g bacon, diced into smallish 1-inch (2.5-cm) cubes
1 garlic bulb, peeled and chopped
2 tablespoon pepper paste
1 tablespoon paprika
1 tablespoon black pepper
3 heaped tablespoons coarse salt
1 cup water

Fresh pork casings

Pound chopped garlic in a mortar and pestle with a pinch of salt.

Season the meat with the garlic paste, paprika and salt (no water). Leave it to rest for 1 to 2 days.

Now add water and liquid pork blood (collected at the time of the slaughter in a container with vinegar). Mix everything well.

Fill a thick pork casing with this mixture, squeezing the meat well. Tie off one end of the sausage with a thin string, making a simple knot. Tie the other end and swing the sausage like a jump rope. Make another simple knot.

Check your sausages for any large air gaps and prick the casing in those areas with a sterilized needle. Ease any air out of the sausage through the pinhole.

To cure the *chouriços*, hang them over a fire for weeks (1 to 5 or 6 weeks). Store the *chouriços* in a cool, dry place

---

Farinheira (Smoked flour sausage)

In Cabeço de Vide there was a large Jewish community, which lived in the Jewish quarter, around Rua Bento Varela. With the arrival of the Inquisition in the 16th century, the Jews were forced to convert or to flee. Some were tried in Évora by the Court of the Holy Office, which condemned them to torture or death. We know that the New-Christians used to make farinheiras *(smoked flour sausages) to deceive their neighbours, who, seeing these sausages in the smokehouse, were convinced that they had really converted and were even eating pork.*

Cubed pork fat
Wheat flour
Garlic, peeled
Coarse salt

Paprika

Casing

In the mortar, crush garlic with salt into a paste. Blanch fat and mix it with the garlic paste, flour and paprika paste. Grind everything through the mincer.

Fill the casing with this mixture and tie the ends with strings to form a ring. Place in the smokehouse for a few days.

Morcela (Black pudding)

The blood of the slaughtered pig was used to make black pudding with the lard (the fat next to the intestines). The pig was hung up after being slaughtered and the blood was collected in a bowl with vinegar to prevent it from coagulating.

Fresh pork meat, cut into small cubes

Fresh pork's blood

Pork fat, cut into small cubes
Onion, peeled and finely chopped
8 garlic cloves, peeled and chopped

Salt
Cumin
Paprika powder

Large intestine casing, well washed

Mix all ingredients ina a pan and bring to the boil with a little water. When it boils, lower the heat, and cook on a low flame. Remove from the heat, add cold water and mix everything very well with your hands until it becomes a consistent dough.

Now prepare the intestine by washing it well with water and lemon. Cut the large intestine into pieces. Sew up one end. Fill, up to ¾ of these sachets with the filling, carefully so they don't burst. Close the other end with a string.

Place the black pudding in a pan with water and cook, keeping the temperature constant but not too high so as not to burst.

Hang on sticks and take to the smokehouse for 3 to 4 days.

Mouros (Smoked meat sausage)

The "mouro" sausage is a smoked sausage. It is made with pork meat trimmings, fat and entrails of the, finely shredded.

Pork shavings
Fat
Guts
Coarse salt
1 garlic bulb, peeled
Sweet paprika
Smoked paprika
Cumin
White wine
Beef casing

In a mortar, crush garlic into a paste. Finely cut the offals, meat shavings and fat into 2 to 2.5 cm pieces.

Mix everything in an earthenware bowl. Add the garlic paste, sweet parika, smoked paprika, cumin, white wine and a little water and mix well.

Leave to rest for 1 to 3 days at a temperature below 10 ° C and humidity of around 80-90%.

After this time, fill the beef casing with the meat mixture, pressing it well. Tie the ends and place in a oak or cork smokehouse for a minimum of 3 days and a maximum of 10 days.

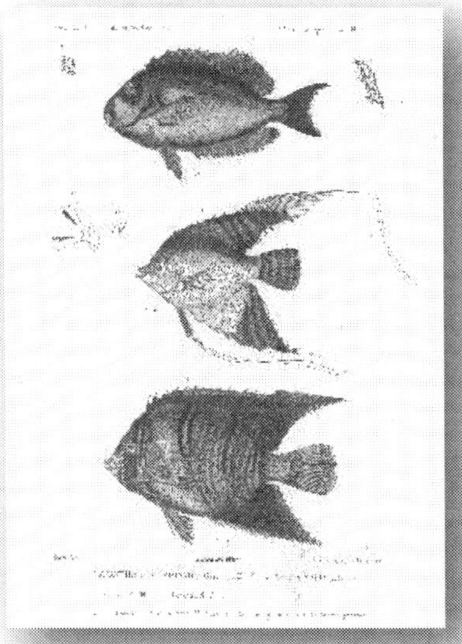

Fish

In the past, it was somewhat difficult to find fresh fish in the Alentejo. The roads were bad, the journey was long, and the fish had to be well packed to arrive in good condition. Some river fish was eaten and, when it appeared on the market, sea fish.

The same didn't happen with salted codfish, which didn't need special care for transportation.

The fish recipes that I present here were the ones that my aunts used to make. In their collection of recipes there were many without title and many without exact indications.

Filetes de corvina (Breaded corvina fillets)

In a shallow bowl or deep plate, marinate the corvina fillets in a mixture of crushed garlic, salt, and vinegar. Prepare 3 shallow dishes: one for flour, one for egg, and one for breadcrumbs. Beat the egg lightly. Dip one fish piece at the time, first in the flour, then in the egg. Let the excess egg drip off before coating the fish in the breadcrumbs. Turn the fish to coat both sides with breadcrumbs. Repeat the process with the remaining fillets. Working in batches, fry the fish in hot oil for about 6 minutes on each side, or until golden brown, crispy, and cooked through. Remove and set on a cooling rack to let drain. Serve with a salad.

Pargo delicioso (Delicious snapper)

1 whole snapper
Salt
2 tablespoons olive oil
Lemon juice
3 onions, peeled and sliced
500 g tomatoes, diced
1 dl milk
2 tablespoons breadcrumbs

For decoration:
Parsley, chopped

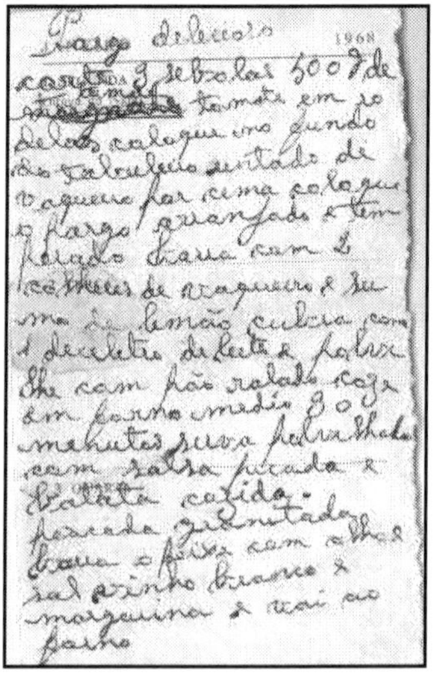
Pargo delicioso 1968

Preheat oven to 180° C. Grease a 2-quart baking dish.

Clean snapper, pat-dry it and season it with salt, olive oil, and lemon juice. Arrange onion and tomato in the bottom of the baking dish. Top with the snapper. Toss breadcrumbs until thoroughly coated.

Bake for 25 to 30 minutes. Sprinkle with chopped parsley and serve with boiled potatoes and salad.

Peixe fidalgo (Nobleman's fish)

Preheat oven to 200°C. Boil fish, green beans and carrots in salted water. Meanwhile, sauté onion in olive oil until tender in a medium saucepan.

Place fish in the bottom of a baking dish and sprinkle fish with the fried onion. Place cooked carrots and green beans around the fish.

Now prepare the sauce. In a saucepan, melt 2 tablespoons butter and whisk in 2 tablespoons flour. Do not brown the mixture. When it starts to thicken, pour in 500 ml milk gradually, stirring constantly. Season with salt and bring to the boil. Stir in egg yolk. Mix well and set aside. Whisk egg white until stiff and carefully add to the sauce.

Pour the sauce over the pre-cooked fish. Bake it until the top is golden brown.

Pescada guarnecida (Baked hake)

A very simple and easy fish recipe.

4 nice hake cuts
4 garlic cloves, peeled
Coarse salt
1 dl white wine
2 tablespoons olive oil

Preheat oven to 180° C.

Crush garlic in a mortar or with a hand blender together with salt, wine, and olive oil and spread it over the fish

Place fish in a baking dish.

Bake for 15 more minutes until the top is golden brown.

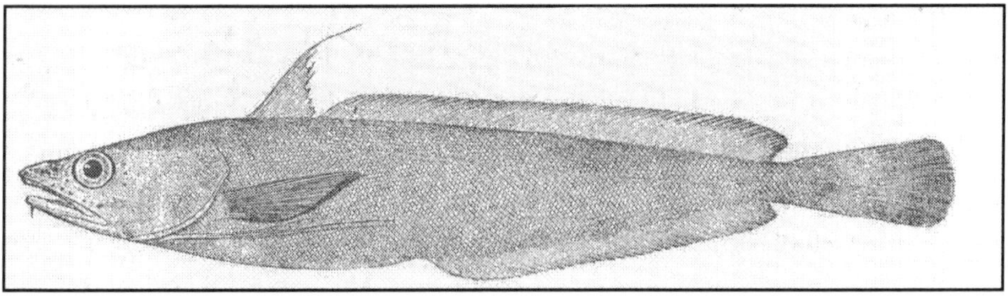

Rissóis de peixe (Fish turnovers)

My Aunts only made fish turnovers when there were leftovers from a fish meal.

For the dough:
Salt
1 cup water
1 lemon rind
1 teaspoon butter
1 cup flour

For the filling
1 tablespoon butter or margarine
1 tablespoon flour
1 dl cold milk
1.5 dl fish stock
Pepper, nutmeg, salt
Leftovers of cooked fish
Parsley, chopped

For the breading:
2 eggs, beaten
Breadcrumbs

For frying:
Oil or olive oil

For the dough, add water, butter, and salt into a saucepan and bring to a boil. Slowly stir in flour and stir quickly with a wooden spoon to form a big dough ball.

Remove dough and reserve until it reaches room temperature.
Now prepare the filling. In a saucepan, melt 2 tablespoons butter and whisk in 2 tablespoons flour. When it starts to thicken, pour in milk, and fish stock gradually, stirring constantly. Season with salt, pepper, and nutmeg and bring to the boil. Stir in fish leftovers and parsley. Mix well and set aside.
To assemble, roll out the cold dough very thinly with a rolling pin. Add about a teaspoon of fish mixture onto dough in one corner leaving enough dough to flip over. Flip the end of the dough up and over the fish mixture. Use a round cutter (or a cup if you don't have a cutter) to cut into half-moon shape turnovers. Repeat the assembly process until you run out of dough. Line a baking tray with cling and line the turnovers down in a single layer without touching.
Prepare 2 shallow dishes: one for egg, and one for breadcrumbs. Dip the turnovers in a beaten egg, then quickly into breadcrumbs, shaking off any excess crumbs. Set aside. Gently place turnovers in sizzling oil and fry until golden brown. Remove onto plate lined with paper towel.

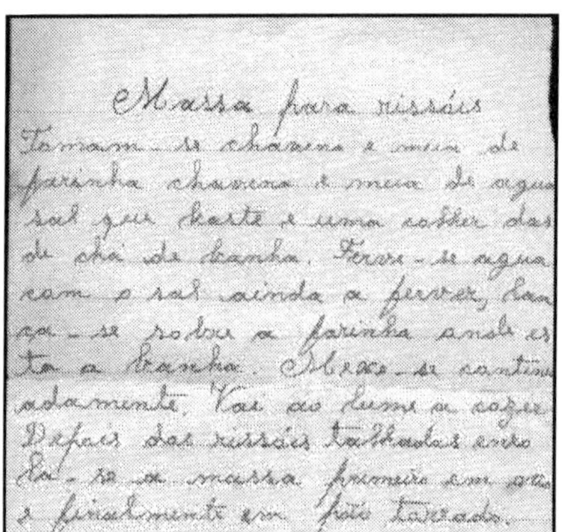
Massa para rissóis
Tomam-se chávena e meia de
farinha chávena e meia de água
sal que baste e uma colher das
de chá de banha. Ferve-se água
com o sal ainda a ferver, lan-
ça-se sobre a farinha onde es-
ta a banha. Mexe-se contínu-
adamente. Vai ao lume a cozer.
Depois dos rissóis talhados envo-
lta-se a massa primeiro em ovo
e finalmente em pão torrado.

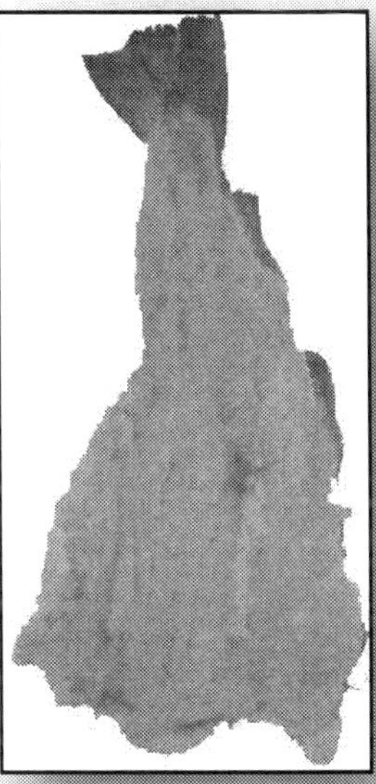

Salted cod

I left most of the codfish recipes just as my Aunties had written them everywhere, in little papers, newspaper pages and booklets.

Amarelo de bacalhau (Cod with eggs)

This recipe is very similar to the cod à brás recipe.

1 dl olive oil
1 onion, peeled and chopped
800 g dried salt cod soaked overnight and shredded
8 eggs, beaten
Salt
400 g fried potato sticks

For the decoration:
Parsley, chopped

Heat olive oil in a heavy, large non-stick skillet over medium-high heat and sauté onion until tender. Mix in shredded cod and potato sticks. Add beaten eggs to the fish mixture in the skillet. Cook over medium heat until eggs are softly set, stirring occasionally, about 3 minutes. Transfer mixture to a platter. Garnish with black olives and the chopped parsley.

Bacalhau andaluz (Andalusian cod)

In my Aunts' recipe collection I found two recipes with very similar names: this one for Andalusian cod and another for Andalusian-style salt cod, with boiled eggs and mayonnaise.

1 large, dried, salted cod cut, soaked overnight and cooked
4 potatoes, peeled, sliced, and fried
2 tablespoons olive oil
2 tablespoons flour
1 onion, peeled and chopped
4 garlic cloves, peeled and chopped
Black pepper
Paprika

1 bunch parsley, chopped
1 egg yolk
3 tablespoons breadcrumbs

Preheat oven to 180° C.

Flake fish, discarding any bones. Reserve the stock.

In a saucepan, heat olive oil and whisk in 2 tablespoons flour. When it starts to thicken, pour in the cod stock gradually, stirring constantly.

In a baking tray, place a layer of the cod flakes and top with a layer of fried potatoes. Repeat until you run out of cod. The last layer is of potatoes.

In a skillet, sauté onion, garlic, parsley, pepper and paprika. Pour over the cod.

Mix egg yolk with breadcrumbs, spread over the sauce and bake until golden brown.

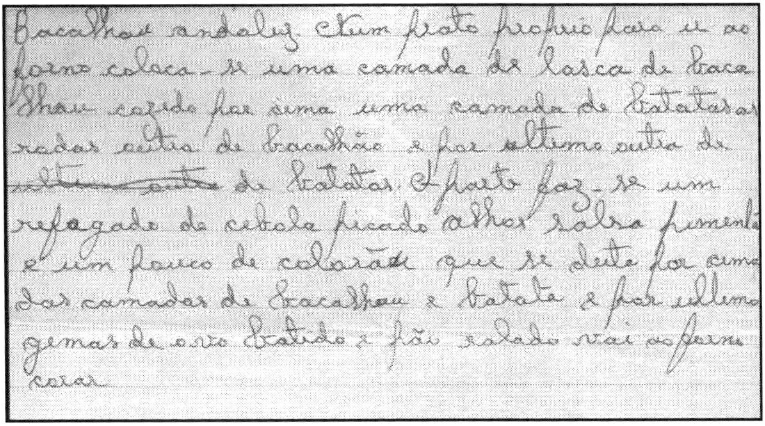
Bacalhau andaluz. Num prato proprio para ir ao
forno coloca-se uma camada de lasca de baca
lhau cozido por cima uma camada de batatas as
radas outra de bacalhão e por ultimo outra de
~~ultimo outra~~ de batatas. A parte faz-se um
refogado de cebola picado alhos salsa pimenta
e um pouco de colorau que se deita por cima
das camadas de bacalhau e batata e por ultimo
gemas de ovo batido e pão ralado vai ao forno
corar

Bacalhau catita (Fancy cod)

Most of my Aunts' codfish recipes were for pies and baked cod.

Cook cod cuts and potatoes in their skins. Meanwhile, prepare a batch of tomato sauce. When cod is cooked, cube the fish, discarding any bones and skin. Peel and slice the potatoes. Mix 2 tablespoons flour with a little water and two egg yolks. Beat the two egg whites until stiff and mix them into the flour mixture. Place the pieces of cod and the potato wheels inside the flour mixture and fry them separately.

Place cod and potatoes in layers in a baking dish, until you run out of cod. Cover everything with the tomato sauce, sprinkle some grated cheese and bake until golden brown.

Bacalhau com chouriço (Cod with smoked sausage)

A good recipe that brings together the timeless cod with the famous Alentejo smoked sausage, chouriço.

Dried, salted cod cut, soaked overnight
Potatoes (double the weight of the cod)
1 onion, peeled and chopped
1 tablespoon pork lard
Thin slices of *chouriço*
1 or 2 garlic cloves, peeled and chopped
Salt
1 whole egg, beaten
Breadcrumbs

Preheat oven to 180 °C. Boil cod and potatoes. Flake fish, discarding any bones. Reserve the stock. Grate potatoes. In a skillet melt lard and sauté onion and garlic. Add *chorizo* and sauté for a few minutes. Add cod and potatoes, mixing everything well. Taste for salt, and if necessary, add some. Place mixture into a buttered baking dish. Pour beaten egg over the mixture. Spread breadcrumbs and bake until golden brown. Serve hot.

Bacalhau frito com molho (Fried cod with sauce)

This recipe, like many others from the little papers I found, was written as follows, without punctuation, which I inserted for better understanding, and without indication of quantities, which I did not add.

Codfish, soaked
Beaten egg
Olive oil
Potatoes, peeled and sliced
Onion, peeled and sliced
Parsley, chopped
Garlic, peeled and crushed
Pepper
Flour
Beaten egg yolks
Lemon juice

Cook soaked salt codfish. Drain and discard any skin and bones, and cut into even-sized pieces. Dip them in beaten egg and then fry them in hot olive oil. Remove. Fry sliced potatoes. Remove. Add onion slices, parsley and garlic. Season with pepper. When onion is soft, add some codfish both mixed with a little bit of flour. When sauce begins to thicken, add cod and potatoes and bring to aboil. Add beaten egg yolks, chopped parsley and lemon juice, stirring quickly to prevent eggs from curdling. Serve hot.

Empadão de bacalhau (Cod casserole)

This recipe had no title in the little paper where it was written.

1 onion, peeled and chopped
2 garlic cloves, peeled and chopped
2 tablespoons olive oil
1 chilli pepper, chopped (optional)
400 g salt cod, soaked, flaked
4 eggs
50 g flour
2.5 dl milk
1.5 kg potatoes, peeled and cut into sticks

Heat oven to 225°C.
Butter an ovenproof dish.
Sauté onion, garlic and chilli in hot olive oil.
Remove from heat and add flaked cod, egg yolks, the flour mixed with the milk and potato sticks. Mix well.
Whip egg whites until stiff and add to the mixture.
Pour mixture into the dish, bake in the pre-heated oven, and bake until nicely golden.

Migas de bacalhau com poejo (Codfish crumb with pennyroyal)

Pennyroyal is the queen of the herbs in the Alentejo, growing wild in the fields. Although it is very popular in the region, my Aunts did not use it very often.

300 g cod, soaked
750 g homemade bread, sliced
Pennyroyal (leaves only)
2 eggs
2 garlic cloves, peeled
1 cup olive oil

Boil cod. Drain and remove skin and bones and shred it. Keep the broth.
Place slices of bread in a bowl and spread the pennyroyal on top. Blanch bread with 1 cup of codfish broth. The bread should be all soaked, but not watery, i.e. make sure there is water visible at the bottom of the bowl. Bring to the boil. As soon as it boils, turn off the heat, cover the pan and leave to soak for 10 minutes.
Add the shredded cod, the eggs and beat everything until you get a mush.
Separately, in a pan, sauté the garlic in hot olive oil. Remove the garlic, add the bread and cod mixture to the olive oil and stir over the heat until it dries out - but do not let it get too dry.

Aunt Maria and aunt Cecília with two of their nieces (1972)

Pastelão de bacalhau (Cod pie)

Another recipe from the Aunts' little book, written without a list of ingredients. I put together the list below.

Codfish, soaked overnight
Onion
Olive oil
Green beans or sprouts
Eggs
Boiled eggs, sliced

For decoration:
Black olives

Boil cod, remove skin and bonés, shred it and sauté it with onion and olive oil. Boil green beans or sprouts, chop them and add them to the sautéed cod, add yolks. Whip egg whites into stiff peaks and add to the cod mixture. Pour into an ovenproof dish. Decorate with slices of boiled egg and bake in the pre-heated oven until the top is nicely golden. Garnish with olives.

Rodelinhas de bacalhau

(Cod rounds)

My Aunts used to make these little rounds of codfish when they had leftovers of boiled or baked cod. They also used to make delicious codfish cakes, but I could not find their recipe.

150 g boiled or baked codfish
50 g margarine
200 g potatoes, boiled
1 egg
1 tablespoon onion, chopped
Parsley, chopped
Salt, pepper, and nutmeg
Flour

Olive oil for frying

Flake cod. Mash potatoes. Mix mash with cod and egg. Add onion and parsley. Season with salt, pepper, and nutmeg.

With flour-dusted hands, form the mixture into walnut-sized balls; flatten.

Place rounds in a frying pan with hot olive oil, and fry in batches. Turn the rounds to fry both sides. Serve with salad.

Meat

Meat is the queen of the Alentejo diet. Pork - excuse me! - is the king, followed by lamb, chicken, and rabbit. Practically everyone had livestock either at home or on the farm.

Arroz de frango (Chicken rice)

My Aunts' chicken rice was not baked in the oven. However, if you want, after the rice is almost cooked, you can decorate it with slices of chorizo, bake in the oven until the rice gets crispy.

100 ml olive oil
1 chicken, cut into pieces
1 onion, peeled and chopped
4 garlic cloves, peeled and minced
Salt to taste
2 cups rice, washed
4 cups water

Fry chicken in hot olive oil in a large ovenproof pan.

Add onion and garlic and season with salt. Reduce heat to low, cover the pan, and stew, for 15 minutes, stirring occasionally.
Add rice. Stir well to combine and add water completely covering the rice. When it starts to boil, reduce heat to low, cover the pan, and again cook, for 15-20 minutes.

If wished, preheat oven to 200 °C. Carefully stir mixture in the pan and flatten slightly using a spatula. Top rice with slices of chorizo. Bake in preheated oven until rice is slightly crisped on top for 10 -15 minutes.

Bife à alentejana (Minced steak)

This "steak à alentejana", which my Aunts used to make, is nothing more than ... a delicious hamburger.

500 g beef steak
80 g *paio,* smoked sausage from pork loin
80 g bacon
Salt and black pepper
All-purpose flour
3 tablespoons margarine

Ground beef, *paio* and bacon, and season with salt and pepper.
Use your hands to form hamburger patties, flatten and coat them in flour. Fry in margarine.

Bifes enrolados (Stuffed steaks)

In the past, very little beef was eaten, but sometimes my Aunts would make these delicious stuffed steaks.

4 flank steaks, wide and thin (if you have thick steaks you must butterfly them, so that they open up like a book)
4 garlic cloves, peeled and crushed
Salt
Pepper
4 hard-boiled eggs
2 tablespoons olive oil

Pound steaks with a meat mallet or a rolling pin to tenderize and flatten. Season meat with garlic, salt, and pepper. Place a hard-boiled egg on top of each steak. Roll up tightly with the stuffing inside like a jelly roll, and tie it up with butcher

twine or a normal string.
Fry rolls in hot olive oil. Once fried, remove the thread, slice perpendicular to the larger egg axes and serve with fricassee sauce

---

Coração de cebolada

(Beef heart stew)

In the past, almost all parts (but the bonés and the skin) of the animals were eaten. These beef heart stew is very tasty. Ask the butcher to trim the heart, remove the fat and cut it into thin steaks.

1 kg beef heart, cut in thin steaks
Coarse salt
Black pepper
5 garlic cloves, peeled and minced
1 tablespoon vinegar
4 onions, peeled and sliced
650 g tomatoes, cubed
2 bay leaves
200 ml olive oil
450 ml dry white wine
3 sprigs of parsley tied with string to a little bundle

Season heart steaks with salt, pepper, garlic, and vinegar

and marinate for at least an hour.

After this time, fry the steaks quickly in hot olive oil. Remove and keep warm.

In the remaining fat, add onion and fry until translucent. Add marinade and a tablespoon of water. Let boil for a while. Pour the sauce over the steaks and serve immediately with potato chips.

Bofes guisados com macarrão (Offal stew with noodles)

Offal is the organs of a butchered animal.

2 tablespoons olive oil
1 onion, peeled and chopped
3 garlic cloves, peeled and minced
Pork offal
Coarse salt and black pepper
Noodles

Heat olive oil. Add onion and garlic and cook until just brown. Add offal and stir fry for a few minutes. Pour in slowly some water and cook over low heat for 2 1/2-3 hours until meat is tender.
Add more water. Bring to the boil. Add noodles and cook for 7-10 minutes.

Borrego assado (Roast lamb)

Easter Sunday dinner is usually roast lamb with potatoes that are baked in the oven in the roast sauce. The side is a salad of shredded lettuce, seasoned with olive oil, salt, and vinegar.

1 leg of lamb, trimmed
1 head garlic, peeled and chopped
1 tablespoon paprika powder
Coarse salt
2 tablespoons red bell pepper paste
125 g lard
4 tablespoons olive oil
2 dl dry white wine
1 onion, peeled and thickly sliced
2 bay leaves
1 bunch parsley
4 large potatoes, peeled and diced

In a mortar, crush garlic, paprika powder, salt, red bell pepper paste, lard, and olive oil. Add wine and rub lamb all over with this mixture. Transfer to a roasting tin and sat on the onion slices. Add bay leaves and parsley and marinate overnight.

The next day, heat oven to 220° C. Roast for 20 minutes. Add potatoes and cook for another 15-20 minutes per 500g (1 hr – 1 hr 20 minutes for 2 kg leg), depending on how pink you like your lamb.

Burras assadas no forno (Baked pork cheeks)

Pork cheeks are known in Alentejo under a funny name: Burras, *female donkeys! They are usually roasted in the oven. .*

6 garlic cloves, peeled
Coarse salt
1 chilli pepper (optional)
1 bay leaf, stemmed and chopped
60 g lard
2 teaspoons olive oil
1 tablespoon red bell pepper paste
1.2 kg pork cheeks
2 onions, peeled and cut into half moons
2.5 dl dry white wine
2 tablespoons vinegar
New potatoes, peeled
Paprika powder

Start by preparing the garlic paste. In a mortar, crush garlic cloves, salt, chilli pepper, and bay leaf. Add lard, olive oil, and paprika.
Coat pork cheeks with garlic paste and leave to rest for a few hours (ideally overnight).
Heat oven to 225 °C.
Cover the bottom of an earthenware baking dish with half-moon onion slices and place pork cheeks on top.

Drizzle with wine and vinegar. Put potatoes around the pork cheeks and sprinkle with a little paprika.
Bake in preheated oven for 25 minutes. Turn the meat over and finish baking for a further 25-30 minutes, until the meat is tender. Drizzle the sauce over the meat every now and then to prevent it from drying out.

Carne de porco frita com migas (Fried pork with *migas*)

This is a very popular dish for Christmas Eve in Alentejo, cooked over an open fire: fried pork with migas *(bread mash). The meat is fried in olive oil, not in lard, so it doesn't get too greasy.*

For the fried pork:
500 g pork steaks
500 g pork leg
4 garlic cloves, peeled
Coarse salt
Flour
Olive oil

For the *migas*, the bread mash:
4 garlic cloves, peeled and sliced
Pingo da carne (the fat from the fried meat)
Sliced stale bread

In a mortar, crush garlic with salt.
Cut pork into 3 to 4 cm cubes and coat with the crushed garlic and salt. Leave it for at least 2 hours.
Lightly cover meat with flour and fry in hot olive oil over a medium heat until golden brown. Remove meat from pan and keep warm.
Now prepare the *migas*.
Heat the fat that is in the pan and fry the garlic. Remove and put aside.
Put the slices of bread in the pan and let them absorb the fat.
Pour in enough water to fully cover the fried bread. Cover the pan and let it simmer over medium heat.
When the water is totally absorbed, whip the bread with a wooden spoon until it becomes crumbly. Form the mash into an oval ball.
Serve the meat with bread mash.

Coelho assado no forno (Roasted rabbit)

In Alentejo everyone used to have a rabbit hutch and those who didn't have hunted wild rabbits that hopped around the fields. Hence there are many rabbit/ hare recipes.

.

2 garlic cloves, peeled and crushed
Coarse salt
1 teaspoon paprika powder
3 tablespoons lard
1 rabbit or hare, kitchen ready and cut into pieces
2.5 dl dry white wine

Crush garlic, salt, paprika, and lard in a mortar.
Wash rabbit, pat dry and rub it with the garlic and lard mixture. Marinate it for a few hours.
Place rabbit into a roasting tin , pour the wine over it and bake in the oven (200 °C) for about 30 –40 minutes, flipping the meat pieces about every 10 minutes. If you' would like the meat to get more color, turn on the grill during the last 5 minutes of the cooking time.

Coelho com molho de cebolada (Rabbit in onion sauce)

There are countless recipes for cebolada *(onion sauce). The writer Eça de Queiroz talks about it in his book "A Cidade e as Serras" ("The City and the Mountains"): "But what impressed her above all was Jacintho's tremendous appetite, the enthusiastic conviction with which he, (...) after numerous steaks in onion saucer, praised our cuisine, swearing he had never ever tasted anything so sublime.*

1 rabbit, kitchen ready and cut into pieces
3 garlic cloves, peeled and chopped
Coarse salt and pepper
1 bay leaf, broken
1 dl vinegar
60 ml olive oil
4 onions, peeled and cut in half-moons
100 ml dry white wine
350 ml water

Season rabbit with garlic, salt, bay leaf, and vinegar. Fry in olive oil and set aside. In the fat in which you fried the rabbit, fry onions. Place a layer of onions and a layer of meat in a pan. Repeat until it is finished. Drizzle with wine and water. Cover pan and bring to a boil. Lower the heat and cook over a medium flame.

Coelho estufado (Rabbit stew)

This recipe can also be prepared with hare.

4 garlic cloves, peeled
Coarse salt
1 medium-sized rabbit or hare, whole
3 tablespoons olive oil
1 dl dry white wine

Crush garlic and salt in a mortar (or with a food processor).
Coat rabbit with the salt and garlic paste. Put olive oil, white wine and 1 dl of water into a large heavy-bottomed pan over a medium heat. When it comes to the boil, add rabbit. Let cook for a few minutes, turn rabbit over and pour another 1 dl of water. Reduce to a simmer, cover and cook on the hob for 60–70 minutes until the rabbit is tender. After 30 minutes, remove the lid to allow the liquid to reduce.

Coelho frito (Fried rabbit)

This is a very common dish both in Cabeço de Vide and in neighbouring towns and villages.

1 rabbit, kitchen-ready and cut into pieces
4 garlic cloves, peeled and chopped
1 onion, peeled and chopped
1 bunch parsley, chopped
1 bay leaf, broken
2 tablespoons red bell pepper paste
2 dl dry white wine
1 dl olive oil
Salt and pepper

Prepare a marinade with onion, garlic, parsley, bay leaf, red pepper paste, and white wine. Add the pieces of rabbit, mix well and leave to marinate overnight.
The next day, fry the rabbit in olive oil in a large heavy-bottomed pan over a medium heat, turning once.

Drizzle the marinade over it and season with salt and pepper. Cover the pan. Bring liquid to a boil over medium-high heat; immediately reduce heat and gently simmer until rabbit is well-done. Serve with diced, fried potatoes.

Costeletas de borrego (Breaded lamb chops)

As a child I loved lamb chops—I think because my Mother even let us eat them by hand!

12 lamb chops

For the marinade:
Juice of 1 lemon
Coarse salt
Pepper, freshly ground
3 garlic cloves, peeled and chopped
1 bay leaf

For the breading:
Fine dry breadcrumbs
2 - 3 beaten eggs

For frying:
Olive oil or vegetable oil

Pound chops with the wooden mallet, season with lemon juice, salt, pepper, garlic, and bay leaf and marinate for 1 hour.
Dip chops in egg; dredge in breadcrumb mixture; dip again in egg.
Heat olive oil in a large skillet over medium heat. Add chops, and cook, turning to brown both sides, until chops are tender.

Cozido de grão (Chickpea stew)

The cozido de grão *is a very popular dish in Alentejo. When the Torre de Palma hotel in Vaiamonte opened, we went to the restaurant for lunch. Almost at the end of the meal, the chef came to our table with a portion of* cozido de grão, *telling us that we had to eat this Alentejo special dish.*

500 g dry chickpeas
1 smoked thin sausage (*linguiça*)
1 smoked flour sausage (*farinheira*)
1 black pudding
500 g bacon
Pork feet
Pork ear
Pork bones
300 g pork (or lamb)
Pork cheek
Pork tongue
200 g green beans, cut into 1 cm rhombuses
3 carrots, peeled and diced
3 potatoes, peeled and diced
Coarse salt (be careful! The sausages already contain salt)
1 bunch fresh mint

Sort chickpeas, wash and soak overnight. The next day, drain and rinse chickpeas.
Cover with water about 5 cm above chickpeas, add

meat and bring to boil on medium heat. Lower heat to simmer and cook until tender, about 1,5 - 2 hours (in a pressure cooker it will take 30 minutes).
Drain. Set meat aside and cut in pieces. Bring liquid to a boil. Add vegetable and cook until tender.
Bring meat back to the pot to get warm. Drain again, put everything in a serving plate, decorate with mint and serve immediately.

Empadas de galinha (Chicken pot pies)

A chicken pot pie made with shortcrust pastry and filled with cooked and shredded chicken is a real treat. If you boil a country chicken, you can prepare the shortcrust pastry with the fat from the broth that solidifies when it cools down.

For the filling:
1 chicken
0.5 smoked pork sausage (*chouriço*)
1 strip smoked bacon
1 garlic clove, peeled
10 peppercorns
1 onion, peeled
1 bunch of herbs, tied (parsley, sage, marjoram)

For the shortcrust pastry:
2 cups flour
1 teaspoon salt
2/3 cup lard
3 tablespoons ice water (or the very cold chicken stock)

For the brush:
1 yolk

Start with the filling. Put all ingredients in a large pot and cover with cold water. Heat and simmer, uncovered, until chicken meat falls off the bones (skim off scum every so often).

Meanwhile make the pastry. Sift the flour with the salt into a large bowl. Add the lard and rub in with your fingertips until the mixture resembles fine breadcrumbs. Stir in a pinch of salt, then add water and mix to a firm dough. Knead the dough briefly and gently on a floured surface. Wrap in cling film and chill while preparing the filling.

Preheat oven to 200 °C.

Remove meat and strain broth. Debone chicken. Cut *chorizo* and bacon into small cubes. Mix everything

together and drizzle with broth.
Roll out the dough, cut out circles and place 1 round in each of the greased regular-size muffin cups. Firmly press in bottom and up side. Fill the moulds with meat. Cut circles of dough to make the tops of the pies, seal edges.
Brush with beaten egg yolk and bake for 20 - 30 minutes or until crust is golden brown.

Ensopado de borrego (Lamb stew)

Easter Sunday lunch usually is lamb stew. For dinner my Aunts used to roast a leg of lamb with potatoes that were baked together with the lamb (s. page 82).

2 kg lamb, cut into pieces
Coarse salt
1 dl olive oil
2 tablespoons lard
2 onions, peeled and chopped
3 garlic cloves, peeled and chopped
1 bunch parsley, chopped
2 bay leaves
1 tablespoon paprika
8 peppercorns
1 cup dry white wine

800 g potatoes, peeled and diced
Stale bread

Rub lamb with salt.
In a large dutch oven or pot over medium-high heat, heat lard. Add lamb and cook on all sides until seared, 10 minutes, working in batches if necessary. Add onion, garlic, bay leaf, parsley, pepper, and paprika and cook until soft, for 5 minutes.
Add wine. Bring to a boil, then reduce heat to a simmer. Season with salt and pepper. Cover and let simmer until lamb is tender, for 30 minutes. Add potatoes and simmer, covered, until potatoes are tender and stew has thickened, for 30 minutes. If it starts to get dry, add drops of hot water, taking care to stir it so it does not stick.
Before you serve, add boiling water in order to soak the bread.
Serve on a deep platter on a layer of very thin slices of stale bread.

Lacão assado no forno (Roast pork leg)

The ideal is to ask the butcher to score the pork leg with a sharp knife in a zig-zag pattern.

1 higher-welfare leg of pork (or another cut but salted and with rind)
1 onion, peeled
6 garlic cloves, peeled
1 bunch parsley
A few leaves of sage and marjoram
2 - 3 egg yolks
Breadcrumbs
Lemon juice

The day before, soak pork leg in cold water to remove salt. The next day, boil pork leg with onion.
Preheat the oven to 225 °C.
Bash garlic, parsley, sage, marjoram, and egg yolks in a pestle and mortar, until you have a paste. When pork leg is tender, remove from pan and rub it with the garlic and herbs paste. Sprinkle with breadcrumbs, place into a large roasting tray and roast for 35 to 40 minutes, or until you have a lovely crisp crackling, then turn oven down to 170°C and slow-cook the leg for 50 to 60 minutes.

Peru assado (Roast turkey)

For Christmas Day, my Aunts always served roast turkey. When I talked to Mrs. Antónia Vicência Frade, she confirmed that this is the dish par excellence of the Christmas Day lunch. When I was a child, I used to find it very funny that my grandfather and then my uncle Heitor would get the turkey drunk with brandy, so that the meat would become more tender. The turkey was only killed when it was already drunk. One Christmas, the turkey never got drunk and escaped the death sentence.

1 small turkey

For the marinade:
Water
1 cup salt
Lemon and oranges, sliced

10 garlic cloves, peeled and crushed
Pepper
Paprika
3 tablespoons margarine
2 dl dry white wine

The day before, prepare a marinade with water, salt, and slices of lemon and orange and pour over the turkey.

The next day, preheat oven to maximum. Bash garlic, pepper, paprika and margarine in a pestle and mortar, until you have a paste. Place the bird on a large roasting tray, rub it all over with the garlic paste and place in the preheated oven and roast for 30 minutes. Turn heat down to 200 °C and roast for another 2 h, or until the juices run clear from the thigh if you pierce it with a knife or a skewer.

When the turkey begins to brown, pour wine over it. Continue basting the turkey with the sauce that forms. At the end, turn heat high to 230 °C to crisp the skin.

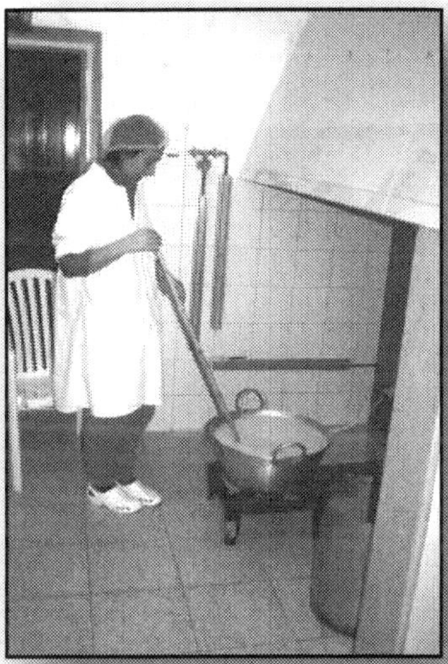

Desserts

Arroz doce (Sweet rice)

The Alentejo sweet rice is white, because it doesn't contain eggs, as in other regions .

1 l milk
1 lemon rind
250 g rice, washed and drained
250 g sugar
Cinnamon

In a large saucepan with water over high heat boil rice for 5 minutes. Drain.

Meanwhile, in another large saucepan over high heat combine milk and lemon rind. When bubbles form at the edges, stir in rice and reduce heat to medium-low. Cook for 60 minutes, stirring often, until rice is tender. Do not

allow to boil.
Add sugar and let it cook on the lowest heat setting for 5 minutes stirring frequently.
Place rice into a serving dish, and top with cinnamon.
Rice will thicken as it cools.

Barriga de freira (Nun's belly)

Monastery sweets often have unappetising names. It is said that the nuns chose these names so as not to draw attention to the richness of their preparations.

500 g sugar
2,5 dl water
200 g stale bread, cubed
12 eggs
25 g butter

In a heavy saucepan over high heat boil water and sugar, until you get a thick syrup (firm-ball stage).

Crumble bread in the food processor. In a bowl, mix crumbled bread and eggs. Add sugar syrup. Put back onto stove top, add butter, and cook slowly until the pudding thickens - don't let it boil! Fill into individual bowls, garnish with cinnamon, and let it cool down.

Encharcada

Encharcada *is a egg-based sweet, from a medieval Alentejo convent. When sugar turned popular, nuns and monks started using the yolks they had in excess (they used the egg whites to iron the priests' vestments and altar cloths and as a purifier for white wine) to make sweet treats.*

370 g sugar
1 dl water
11 egg yolks
2 egg whites

In a heavy saucepan over high heat boil water and sugar, until you get a thick syrup (firm-ball stage). In the meantime, whisk yolks and eggs whites in a bowl.

Using a ladle, press the eggs and yolks through a fine-mesh sieve into the candy syrup. While stirring, cook until small curds form and mixture is very thick and appears slightly curdled.

Transfer to a serving plate. Guide the flame of a blow-torch back and forth over the top of the desert until the surface caramelizes. (Alternatively, place under oven broiler.)

Farófias (Poached meringues)

It is not clear where this recipe comes from. The nuns of the Convent of Nossa Senhora da Conceição, in Loulé, prepared a sweet, called Nuvens *Clouds), in a very similar way to* farófias. *Carlos Bento da Maia, in his book "Tratado Completo de Cozinha e de Copa", published in 1904, presents a recipe for* farófias *(page 538), which begins by saying "this desert is generally made to make use of the egg whites leftovers from the preparation of other puddings.*

4 eggs
5 dl milk
Lemon rind
1 tablespoon + 150 g sugar
2.5 tablespoons cornstarch
4 egg yolks
Ground cinnamon

Beat 4 egg whites to soft peaks, then add 1 tablespoon sugar, beating all the while. Continue until stiff glossy peaks form.

In a saucepan on medium to low heat, pour in milk and lemon rinds. When it comes to the boil, drop meringue in by rounded tablespoons. Poach the meringues for 1 - 2 minutes in the milk, then turn and poach the other side for 1 - 2 minutes. With a skimmer, transfer them to a bowl. Set aside.

As soon as all meringues are poached, strain milk and mix in remaining sugar. Add corn starch, dissolved in a little cold milk, and cook, stirring constantly, over medium to low heat until slightly thickened.

Remove from heat, add egg yolks and cook, stirring constantly, over low heat for a few minutes.

Pour the custard over the meringues and sprinkle with ground cinnamon.

Serve chilled.

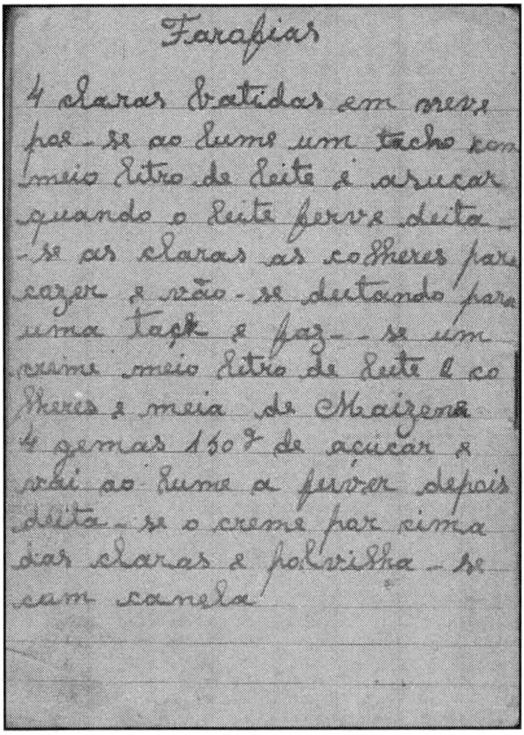

Farofias

4 claras batidas em neve
põe-se ao lume um tacho com
meio litro de leite e açucar
quando o leite ferve deita-
-se as claras às colheres para
cozer e vão-se deitando para
uma taça e faz-se um
creme meio litro de leite e co
lheres e meia de Maizena
4 gemas 150 g de açúcar e
vai ao lume a ferver depois
deita-se o creme por cima
das claras e polvilha-se
com canela

Leite creme (Crème brûlée)

Mrs Antónia Vicência Frade told me a sweet story. As a child she heard about a friend who was very ill and did not want to eat anything. She was very upset and when she got home she asked her mother to make something for her friend to eat. And her mother made her some crême brûlée which, in fact, her school friend ate.

0.5 l milk
1 cinnamon stick
1 lemon rind
6 egg yolks
2 teaspoons corn starch
200 g sugar
4 tablespoons caster sugar

Place milk, lemon rind, and cinnamon stick into a saucepan and slowly bring to the boil. Remove from heat. Meanwhile, beat together egg yolks, corn starch, and sugar until light and fluffy. Add egg yolk mixture into the milk, whisking continuously. Return to heat until the mixture thickens and forms a cream, stirring continuously.
Divide mixture between 4 ramekins. Allow to cool.
To serve, sprinkle each *crème brûlée* with a tablespoon of caster sugar and caramelize under a very hot grill or using the chef's torch.

Pudim de requeijão
(Cottage cheese pudding)

Cottage cheese is a curd cheese product made by draining the cheese, as opposed to pressing it, retaining some of the whey and keeping the curds loose.

500 g sheep's cottage cheese
3 eggs
12 egg yolks
1 tablespoon butter
Lemon rind
125 g sugar

Preheat oven to 160 °C.
Grease a deep baking pan.
Mix together cottage cheese and egg yolks. Add butter, lemon rind, and sugar.
Whisk egg whites until stiff; fold into cheese mixture.
Place mixture into baking pan. Place dish in pan of water. Bake for 50 minutes.

Pudim de toucinho (Lard pudding)

Alentejo is famous for its pork, from which everything is used - for sweet and savoury dishes. In this case, we have a sweet lard pudding.

For the caramel:
80 g sugar

For the pudding:

500 g lard, desalted
500 g honey
9 egg yolks
1 tablespoonful ground cinnamon

Preheat oven to 200 °C.

Start with the caramel. In a large heavy saucepan, cook and stir sugar over low heat until sugar is melted and golden. Pour into a pudding tin, tilting to coat bottom of each cup; let stand for 10 minutes.

For the pudding, melt lard, squeeze very well, and strain the drippings. Melt honey and mix it with the cooled dripping. Beat egg yolks, add cinnamon and the honey-dripping mixture. Bring to a boil and cook for a few minutes.
Pour over caramelized sugar. Pour very hot water in a pan. Bake for 30 minutes, or until a knife inserted in the centre comes out clean, 40-45 minutes.

Sopa dourada (Golden soup)

*The "golden soup" is actually a Portuguese dessert served throughout the country and, however, with some differences, which characterise the region. In Alentejo, for example, we use fried bread, almonds and white squash (*gila*) jam.*

100 g stale bread, cubed
Oil for frying
150 g *gila* (white squash jam)
10 egg yolks
500 g sugar
300 ml water
100 g almonds, peeled and grated

For the decoration
Ground cinnamon

Fry bread in very hot oil. Drain well.
Mix *gila* jam with egg yolks.
In a heavy saucepan over high heat boil water and sugar, until you get a thick syrup (firm-ball stage). In the meantime, whisk yolks and eggs whites in a bowl. Add *gila*-yolks misture and cook for a few minutes.

Add almond and cook for a few minutes. Finally, add fried bread and cook, stirring continually. Place on a plate and sprinkle with ground cinnamon. Serve cold.

Cakes and cookies

Almendrados (Almond cookies)

These cookies are popular all over the country, but their origin is from the South.

1 egg white
250 g brown sugar
200 g almonds, peeled and finely sliced
2 tablespoons flour

Preheat oven to 180° C. In a mixing bowl, beat egg whites to a stiff peak. Add sugar, almonds, and flour, mixing thoroughly. *Place* spoonfuls of the dough on a greased cookie sheet. Bake for approximately 20 minutes until cookies turn a golden colour.

Argolas meladas (Fried dough rings)

Every time we would visit our Aunts, they would make us these fried rings covered with syrup.

6 eggs
12 tablespoons suet
12 tablespoons brown sugar
4 cl brandy
Lemon peel
Ground cinnamon
Flour
1 teaspoon baking powder
Olive oil or vegetable oil for frying

For the syrup:
1 kg white sugar
0.5 l water

Beat eggs, sugar, suet, and brandy in a bowl. Add lemon peel, ground cinnamon, flour, and baking powder. Knead until the dough no longer sticks to your hands. Wet your fingers. Heat oil in a deepfrying pan. Grab a small handful of dough and stretch it into a ring, then toss the dough quickly into the oil. Cook briefly, 20 seconds or so, and then flip the doughnuts using the handle of a long wooden spoon. Cook the rings in the oil until they are golden brown, then remove them to a paper towel-lined plate. Meanwhile, prepare the syrup. Place sugar and water in a large saucepan and bring to a boil, stirring, Lower heat and simmer for 15 minutes, or until mixture thickens slightly. Drizzled the rings with the warm syrup.

Argolas mimosas (Sweet rings)

There are many popular recipes for sweet rings, with or without syrup, with or without sugar and cinnamon on top.

500 g brown sugar
3 eggs
60 g margarine, at room temperature
1 pinch of salt
1 teaspoon ground cinnamon
1 kg flour (approximately)

Preheat oven to180 °C. Line a baking tray with parchment paper.
Beat sugar, eggs, margarine, salt and cinnamon. Slowly add flour.
Wet your fingers. Grab a small handful of dough and stretch it into a ring, then place on the baking tray. Bake until the rings are golden brown.

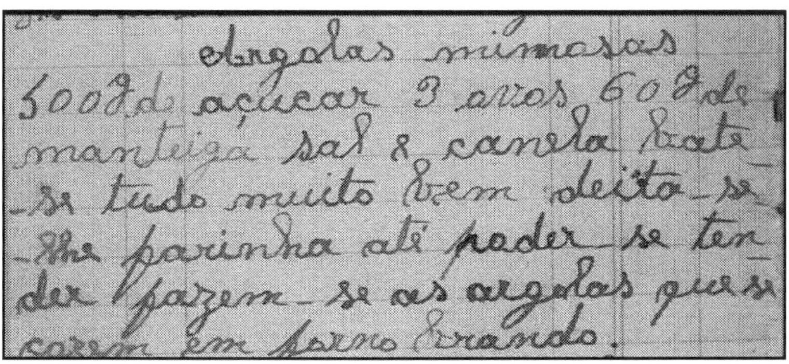
Argolas mimosas
500g d açucar 3 ovos 60g de
manteiga sal e canela bate-
-se tudo muito bem deita-se
-lhe farinha até poder se ten-
der fazem-se as argolas que se
cozem em forno brando.

Azevias
(Fritters with chickpea filling)

These fritters are a popular dessert for Christmas. The filling is made of chickpeas and almonds.

For the dough:
500 g flour
1 tablespoon olive oil
90 g suet
Warm water
Salt

For the filling:
500 g cooked chickpeas (you can use a tin/glass)
500 g sugar
8 egg yolks
Rind of 2 lemons

Start with the dough. Knead all ingredients together. If needed, add some water. Set the dough in the fridge until you are finished with the filling.

For the filling, drain chickpeas, and purée.
In a heavy saucepan over high heat boil water, lemon rind, and sugar, until you get a thick syrup (firm-ball stage).

Add chickpeas puree and cook, stirring continually, until you get a thick syrup (firm-ball stage). Add egg yoks and cook for a few minutes.

Now roll the dough thinly on your workplace which should be sprinkled with some flour. Cut rings using the edge of a glass, or mug. Put a tablespoon of a filling and close dough rings forming half-moons. Fry in hot oil, sprinkle with sugar and ground cinnamon.

Boleima de massa (Yeast dough cake)

Boleima is a simple cake: leavened dough with ground cinammon and sugar!

1 kg bread dough (yeast dough)
2.5 dl olive oil
1 dl milk
250 g brown sugar
2 eggs
1 teaspoon ground cinnamon
1 kg flour

For decoration:
Sugar
Ground cinnamon

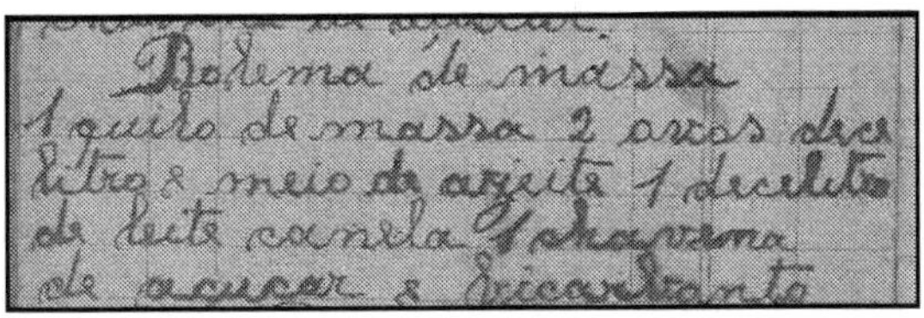
Boleima de massa
1 quilo de massa 2 ovos deci
litro e meio de azeite 1 decilitro
de leite canela 1 chavena
de açucar e bicarbonato

Mix bread dough, olive oil, sugar, eggs, cinnamon and flour. Knead well.
Preheat oven to 200 °C. Line a baking tray with parchment paper.
Pour the batter onto the tray and leave to rest for 20 to 30 minutes.
Sprinkle generously with sugar and cinnamon. Bake until a toothpick inserted into the centre of the tray comes out dry.
Turn out onto a rack and leave to cool. Cut into squares.

Boleima de torresmos (Yeast dough crackling cake)

This fusion sweet-salty might seem strange, but it works perfectly in this popular Alentejo cake.

1 kg bread dough (yeast dough)
250 g brown sugar
1 tablespoon ground cinnamon
2 eggs
1 cup cracklings, finely diced
All purpose flour

Mix bread dough, sugar, eggs, cinnamon. Add cracklings and flour. Knead well.
Preheat oven to 200 °C. Line a baking tray with parchment paper.
Pour the batter onto the tray and leave to rest for 20 to 30 minutes.
Sprinkle generously with sugar and cinnamon. Bake until a toothpick inserted into the centre of the tray comes out dry.
Turn out onto a rack and leave to cool. Cut into squares.

Bolo da tia Cecília (Cake)

My Aunts used to make us this wonderful simple cake, that we would take to the Camões estate. My sister and I would lay down on a woolen blanket in the shade and read while the Aunts would work in the fields. And at snack time we used to eat the cake!

180 g brown sugar
3 eggs
100 g softened margarine
4 cl Port wine
Ground cinnamon
180 g all-purpose flour
3 teaspoons baking powder

Preheat oven to 180 °C. Lightly grease an angel food cake pan (tube pan).

Beat sugar and eggs, until it thickens. Add margarine, Port wine, and cinnamon. Beat for a few minutes. Add flour and baking powder, and beat on medium speed until completely combined.

Pour or spoon the mixture into the tin, smooth the top and bake on the middle shelf of the oven, until the cake looks well risen and golden.

Bolo de água (Water cake)

Another delicious family cake

4 eggs
3 cups sugar
1 cup water
1 lemon, juice and zest
3 cups all purpose flour
1 tablespoon baking powder

Preheat oven to 180 °C.
Lightly grease an angel food cake pan (tube pan).
Whisk egg whites until stiff.
Sift flour, sugar, baking powder, and salt into a large bowl.
Using an electric mixer on high speed, beat yolks and sugar until light and fluffy.
Add water, lemon juice and zest, flour, and baking powder, beat on medium speed until completely combined.
Carefully fold in egg whites.
Pour into the prepared cake pan and bake for about 40-30 minutes, or until a toothpick inserted in center of cake comes out clean.

Bolo de água mel (Molasses cake)

Água mel (*honey molasses) is a by-product of honey that is only found in the Alentejo and Algarve. It is obtained from the slow boiling of the water resulting from washing the waxes after extracting the honey.*

6 eggs
3 cups brown sugar
1 cup milk
1 cup oil
1 cup *água mel* (honey molasses)
3 cups flour
3 teaspoons baking powder
1 teaspoon ground cinnamon
Zest of 1 lemon

Preheat oven to 180 °C. Lightly grease an angel food cake pan (tube pan), and dust it with flour. Shake off the excess. Whisk egg whites until stiff. Using an electric mixer on high speed, beat yolks and sugar until light and fluffy. Add milk and oil and beat on medium speed until completely combined. Add *água mel*, lemon zest and slowly flour and baking poder, and cinnamon. Carefully fold in egg whites. Pour into the prepared cake pan and bake for about 60 minutes, or until a toothpick inserted in center of cake comes out clean. Leave to cool in the tin.

Bolo de mel (Honey cake)

Alentejo honey is multifloral and very good.

2 tablespoons honey
250 g brown sugar
1 cup olive oil
4 eggs
1 cup milk
250 g of flour
1 teaspoon bicarbonate
1/2 teaspoon ground cinnamon
1/2 teaspoon ground aniseed

Preheat oven to 200 °C.
Lightly grease an angel food cake pan (tube pan) and sprinkle with flour. Shake off the excess.

Mix honey and sugar. Add egg yolks and olive oil and whisk very well.

Pour in milk and add flour, bicarbonate, cinnamon, and aniseed. Beat on medium speed until completely combined..

Whisk egg whites until stiff and carefully fold in into the batter.

Pour into the prepared cake pan and bake for about 40 minutes, or until a toothpick inserted in center of cake comes out clean.

Bolo finto (Leavened cake)

Fintar *means to rise. The* bolo finto, *which is eaten at Easter; is thus a cake that has to rise, to be leavened. It is made with bread dough, flavoured with fennel seeds and cinnamon. The lard is used to keep it longer resh .*

4.5 - 6 dl water
3 tablespoons fennel seeds
1 cinnamon stick
25 g fresh yeast
1 kg all purpose flour
300 g brown sugar
200 g lard
100 g margarine, melted

For the brush:
1 egg, beaten

Place water, fennel seeds, and cinnamon stick in a saucepan over high heat and bring to the boil. Turn off the knob, but keep the pan on the heat until it is lukewarm.
Drain. Crumble fresh yeast into the flavoured water and stir until dissolved..
Place flour in a large bowl and make a well in the middle. Give the yeast mixture to the flour, add the rest of the ingredients and mix well. Knead well using the kneading attachments of your mixer or with your hands.

Cover with a clean kitchen cloth and let the dough rise in a warm place. It should double in size.
Take the dough out of the bowl, shape round cakes and place them on a tray dusted with flour. Do not place them too close together as they will rise. Cover the cakes with a cloth and let them rise again.
Preheat oven to 200 °C.
Using scissors, cut the tops of each cake crosswise so that they have all 4 spouts. Brush the cakes with beaten egg and bake in the oven for 40 minutes.

Bolo podre (Rotten cake)

The bolo podre*, a delicious cake from Alentejo, was probably created in a monastery and, like other conventual sweets, has a name that reminds something bad. Some people think that the name comes from the fact that it keeps for a long time - until it becomes "rotten"?*
It might have been created by the nuns of the

Nossa Senhora da Esperança Convent, in Vila Viçosa, founded in 1541. In those days it was prepared with "rolão" *flour (flour with bran). Like most cakes in Alentejo, it takes spices, cinnamon and cloves.*
When I was a child, I did not like this cake because of its strong taste of honey and spices, but now I love it exactly because it tastes of honey and spices.
My Aunts' recipe uses baking soda, but I prefer to use baking powder. It is advisable to grease the pan with olive oil so that the flavour of the cake is not adulterated with the flavour of another fat.

7 eggs
500 g brown sugar
1 dl olive oil
2 tablespoons honey
0.5 dl brandy
1 teaspoon ground fennel
1 teaspoon ground cinnamon
Peel and juice of 1 orange
250 g flour
1 teaspoon baking powder

Preheat oven to 180 °C.
Lightly grease with olive oil an angel food cake pan (tube pan) and sprinkle with flour. Shake off the excess.
Whisk egg whites until stiff.
Beat egg yolks and sugar until light and fluffy. Add olive oil, honey, brandy, zest of the orange peel, cinnamon,

and fennel. Beat on medium speed until completely combined.
Add flour and baking powder and beat for 10 minutes if using an electric mixer (if you beat by hand, you should beat for 1 hour. This cake must be very well beaten).
Fold in the egg whites.

Pour into the prepared cake pan and bake for about 40 minutes, or until a toothpick inserted in centre of cake comes out clean.

Borrachões (Drunkies)

These doughnuts got their name because of the large amount of brandy they contain: 1 cup! They're made at Carnival - it's Carnival, everything is allowed.

2 dl olive oil or lard
2 dl brandy
Salt
650 g flour
200 g brown sugar

For frying:
Olive oil or vegetable oil

For decoration:
Sugar
Ground cinnamon

Mix brandy with olive oil (or lard) and salt and gradually add flour and sugar. Mix well.
When it is elastic and quite pliable, let it rest for 20 - 30 minutes.
Flour the working surface and roll out the dough with a rolling pin until it is very thin. With a round biscuit cutter, cut into circles. With a thimble remove the centre.
Line 1-2 baking sheets with parchment paper. Place doughnuts onto the lined baking sheet and allow to rest as the oil is being heated.
Place a cooling rack with kitchen paper over another baking sheet.
Working in batches, fry for 1 – 2 minutes on each side. Carefully remove from the oil and place onto prepared rack. Repeat with remaining doughnuts. Drizzle with sugar and ground cinnamon.

Filhoses (Crispy fried dough)

At my Aunts' house we used to have filhoses *at Christmas and Carnival. I love these very thin, and crispy fried dough.*

3 eggs
75 g sugar
A pinch of salt
2 tablespoons lard
1 tablespoon rum or cognac
Flour

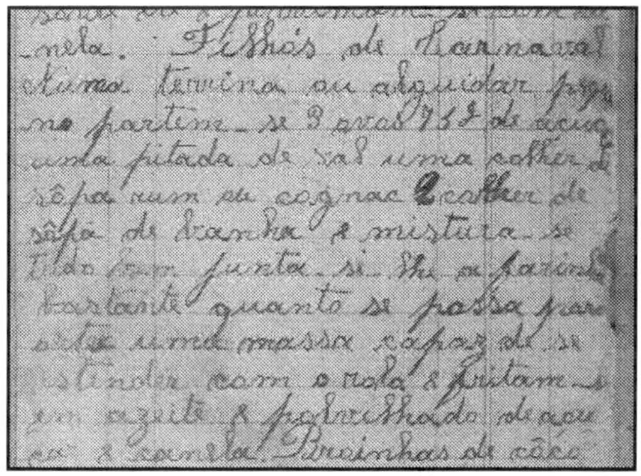

nela. Filhós de Carnaval
Numa terrina ou alguidar peque-
no parte-se 3 ovos 75 g de açúc-
ar uma pitada de sal uma colher de
sôpa rum ou cognac 2 colher de
sôpa de banha e mistura-se
tudo bem junta-se-lhe a farinha
bastante quanto se possa para
obter uma massa capaz de se
estender com o rolo e fritam-se
em azeite e polvilhado de açu-
car e canela. Broinhas de côco

For frying:
Olive oil or vegetable oil

For decoration:
Sugar
Ground cinnamon

Beat eggs, sugar, salt, lard, rum (or cognac) in a small bowl. Gradually add enough flour until you have a dough that can be rolled out with a rolling pin.
Flour the working surface and roll out the dough with a rolling pin until it is very thin. Cut into squares, making a few cuts in the middle.
Fry in very hot olive oil for 1 – 2 minutes on each side. Carefully remove from the oil, drain, and place onto a tray with kitchen paper. Repeat with remaining dough. Drizzle with sugar and cinnamon.

Filhoses de forma
(Shaped fried dough)

When I was little child I used to love watching my Aunts make these fritters, using a metal mould (the one I liked best was butterfly-shaped), attached to a long, thin handle. There are two tips: heat the vegetable oil with the mould inside and, when dipping the mould into the batter, be careful not to go over the height of the mould.

4 eggs
250 g flour
50 g brown sugar
2.5 dl milk
Peel and juice of 1 orange
4 cl brandy
Salt

For frying:
Vegetable oil

For sprinkling:
Sugar
Ground cinnamon

Using an electric mixer on high speed, beat all ingredients on medium speed until completely combined.
Heat oil with the mould inside.

Remove mould, shake off the excess oil, dip in the batter, taking care not to go over the height of the mould, and fry until the dough comes loose, naturally. Turn and fry the other side.
Remove from the oil, drain on kitchen paper, and drizzle with sugar and cinnamon.

Filhoses de forma (Rolled fried dough)

At Carnival, the tables are full of fritters. The fried dough - of different kinds - is prepared on the Thursday of the week before Carnival.

500 - 750 g all purpose flour
Salt
6 eggs
1 tablespoon lard
1 tablespoon butter, at room temperature
3 cl brandy
1 tablespoon sugar
Peel and juice of 1 orange

For the syrup:
1 kg sugar
2,5 dl water

Sift flour into a bowl. Make a well in the centre. Add eggs one at a time, salt, lard, butter, brandy, zest and orange juice. Knead until you have an elastic dough.
Flour the working surface and roll out the dough with a rolling pin until it is very thin. Cut into wide strips (approximately 20 cm long and 7 cm wide). Roll the end of the strip in the tines of a long fork, dip in plenty of very hot oil, and fry in very hot olive oil for 1 – 2 minutes on each side until golden brown. Carefully remove from the oil, drain, and place onto a tray with kitchen paper. Repeat with remaining strips.
Now prepare the syrup. In a heavy saucepan over high heat boil water and sugar, until you get a thick syrup (firm-ball stage). Drizzle the syrup over the fritters (or, if you prefer, sprinkle with sugar and cinnamon). Some people only sprinkle honey over them.

Folar da Páscoa (Easter nests)

During Holy Week, folares *are prepared. On Easter Sunday the children give them to their godmothers. The* folares *are decorated with hard-boiled eggs, stuck together with dough in a cross shape.*

4,5 dl water
1.5 dl brandy
3 tablespoons fennel seeds

Lemon rind
1 cinnamon stick
25 g fresh yeast
1 kg flour
300 g brown sugar
200 g lard
3 eggs

For decoration:
6 to 8 hard-boiled eggs
2 beaten eggs

Place water, fennel seeds, and cinnamon stick in a saucepan over high heat and bring to the boil. Turn off the knob, but keep the pan on the heat until it is lukewarm.
Drain. Crumble the fresh yeast into the flavoured water and stir until dissolved.
Place flour in a large bowl and make a well in the middle. Give the yeast mixture to the flour, add the rest of the ingredients, and mix well. Knead well using the kneading attachments of your mixer or with your hands.
Cover with a clean kitchen cloth and let the dough rise in a warm place. It should double in size.
Take the dough out of the bowl, shape round cakes, and place them on a tray dusted with flour. Do not place them too close together as they will rise. Keep a little dough to hold the eggs in.
Place a hard-boiled egg in the centre of each cake. Hold the eggs with two cross-shaped dough rolls.
Cover the cakes with a cloth and let them rise again.
Preheat oven to 200 °C.

Brush the cakes with beaten egg and bake in the oven for 30 - 40 minutes.

Fritos de mogango (Pumpkin fritters)

You have to drain the cooked pumpkin very well, before adding it into the dough.

500 g pumpkin, peeled
Salt
3 eggs
1 tablespoon brown sugar
Peel and juice of 2 oranges
1 teaspoon ground cinnamon
Flour
1 tablespoon baking powder

For sprinkling:
Ground cinnamon
Sugar

For frying:
Vegetable oil

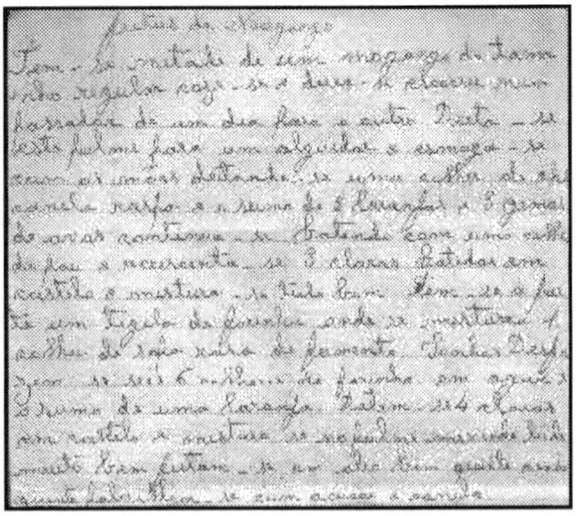

In a pan over high heat boil pumpkin in water and salt. Drain very well (for example, leave overnight).

Whisk egg whites until stiff.
Place the cooked pumpkin into a bowl and mash it with your hands. Add egg yolks, sugar, zest and orange juice, and cinnamon. Mix well.
Fold in the egg whites. Gradually add flour and baking powder until you have a thick dough.
Heat oil. Using a tablespoon put the batter into the oil. When the sides are getting golden, flip them. Remove from oil with a slotted spoon and drain on kitchen paper, so that more excess oil can be absorbed while you go through the other batches. Drizzle with some sugar and cinnamon.

Manéis (Muffins)

These were my favourite muffins and my Aunts always made them for me when I visited them on the summer holidays. In the afternoon, I would lie under a fig tree reading and eating manéis.

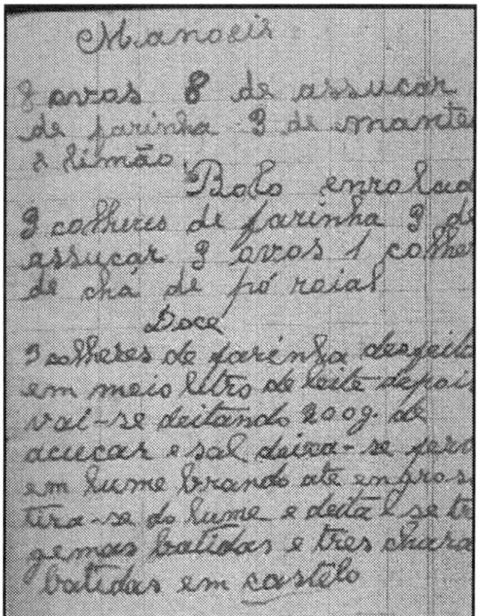

Manoeis
8 ovos 8 de assucar
de farinha 8 de mante
e limão
Bolo enrolad
8 colheres de farinha 8 de
assucar 8 ovos 1 colher
de chá de pó reial
Doce
8 colheres de farinha desfeita
em meio litro de leite depois
vai-se deitando 200g. de
acucar e sal deixa-se ferv
em lume brando ate engros
tira-se do lume e deita-se te
gemas batidas e tres claras
batidas em castelo

8 eggs
450 g sugar
170 g butter, at room temperature
Lemon zest

225 g flour

Preheat oven to 175° C. Lightly grease or line with paper liners muffin cups.
Whisk egg whites until stiff.
Sift the flour and baking powder into a small bowl.
Using an electric mixer on high speed, beat yolks and sugar until light and fluffy.
Add butter and lemon zest.
Stir in flour mixture just to combine. Carefully fold in egg whites.
Divide the batter evenly between the muffin cups and bake for 15 minutes. The muffins are done when a toothpick inserted into the centre comes out with only a few moist crumbs attached.

Nógado

One of the popular sweets at Carnival in Alentejo is nógado, *made with fried dough, cut in triangles. The origin of this recipe is the Royal Convent of the Maids in Borba. My mother, who comes from Ribatejo, learnt to prepare with my Aunts and often made it, although it takes a long time to prepare. Mrs. Antónia Vicência's mother always added a handful of sugar to the honey so that the fried dough would better bind to the syrup.*

8 eggs
5 dl olive oil or lard
Salt
Flour until tender

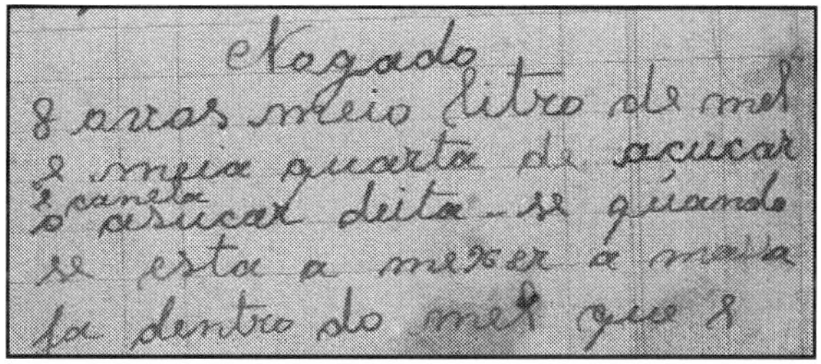
Nogado
8 ovos meio litro de mel
e meia quarta de açucar
e canela o açucar deita-se quando
se esta a mexer a massa
la dentro do mel que 8

For the syrup:
5 dl honey
2,5dl sugar
1 cinnamon stick
Lemon rind

For frying:
Olive oil

Using an electric mixer on high speed, beat eggs, olive oil and salt very well. Add enough flour to form dough.
With your hands form "sausages" (thin rolls with 1cm diameter) and cut them into pieces about 1cm long.
Heat olive oil and fry the "sausages".
Meanwhile, prepare the syrup. In a heavy saucepan over high heat boil honey and sugar, a little water, cinnamon, and lemon rind, until you get a thick syrup (soft-ball stage). Remove lemon rind and cinnamon stick.
Gradually introduce the fried pieces of dough in the syrup, let it cook and set aside. The "sausages" turn golden and the honey dries.
Wet your hands, make piles with the fried dough that has been soaked in the syrup, compress them, and place them on orange or lemon leaves.
Place the dough on a board, make a layer and let it dry.
With a hot knife, cut triangles.

Quadrados de laranja (Orange squares)

My Aunts used to bake these orange squares in the wintertime, the orange season, for our snacks. Our Aunts spoiled us a lot!

2 eggs
100 g butter, at room temperature
180 g sugar
180 g flour
1 teaspoon baking powder
Zest of 2 oranges

For the syrup:
250 g sugar
Juice of 2 oranges

Preheat oven to 180 °C. Grease a baking pan or line with parchment paper. Whisk egg whites until stiff. Sift the flour and baking powder into a bowl.

Using an electric mixer on high speed, beat butter and sugar until light and fluffy.

Add flour and baking powder and orange zest, beat on medium speed until completely combined. Carefully fold in egg whites.

Pour into the prepared baking pan and bake until a toothpick inserted in centre of cake comes out clean. Meanwhile, prepare the syrup by mixing sugar and

orange juice.
Leave the cake in the tray, cut it into small squares, and drizzle with the syrup. Leave it in the tray overnight.

Queijinhos do céu (Heaven cookies)

I'm not sure if these cookies were originally from Cabeço de Vide, but they were always made in the house of Mrs. D. Antónia Vicência Frade. The passinhas *are made in the same way, but with the addition of melted chocolate and a little butter to the dough, giving it the shape of a fig sultana.*

250 g sugar
250 almonds, peeled and grated
Ovos moles (Sweet eggs paste)

In a heavy saucepan over high heat boil water and sugar, until you get a thick syrup (thread stage).

Remove from the knob and add almonds. Leave to cool. Take small pieces of dough and make a small ball. With a finger, make a small hole in the middle where you put a little sweet eggs paste. Close the ball.
Use your hands to shape it into a little round cookie. Sprinkle with sugar and place on a serving plate.

The two oldest nieces (1958)

Jams

Compota de pêssego (Peach jam)

In the summer, my Aunts used to make peach jam that they kept in jars on the cupboard. I used to love to go there to "steal" jam with a big spoon or eat it with maria biscuits.

1 kg peaches
Juice of 1 lemon
500 g sugar
1.5 dl water

Peel peaches, cut them into pieces and drizzle with lemon juice.

In a heavy saucepan over high heat boil water and sugar for 2 minutes. Add peaches and cook them for a few minutes.
Remove peaches from the pan and place them in the jam pot.
Continue to boil the syrup over high heat, until it reduces by half. Pour over the peaches.

Doce de abóbora chila (White squash jam)

In former days, this white squash could not be cut with a knife, because it would oxidate and the jam would turn dark. The squash used to be thrown to the ground. Nowadays all knives are made of stainless steel, so you can cut the chila *squash using a knive.*

500 g de *chila* (white squash)
600 g de caster sugar
800 g de water

Cut squash into pieces. Wash it, remove the seeds, place it in a big pan, cover it with water and boil it. When the rind comes off, remove squash, place it in a large bowl with cold water, discard the rind and any remaining seeds and break it up with your hands.

Season water with salt and leave the squash in the salted water for 24 hours. Drain, squeezing the squash very well.

In a heavy saucepan over high heat boil water and sugar. After a while, add the cooked *chila* and boil again, until you get a thick syrup (firm-ball stage).

Remove from the heat and spoon into jam jars, close and process the jars (boiling the closed jar and its contents for at least 10 minutes).

Doce de figos (Fresh fig jam)

My Aunts had fig trees in both farms. As figs are a very sweet fruit, less sugar is used than for other jams.

1 kg fresh figs, stemmed and cut into small pieces
750 g sugar

In a large saucepan, toss the fig pieces with the sugar and let stand, stirring occasionally, for 3 hours, until the sugar is mostly dissolved and the figs are juicy.

Bring to a boil, stirring until the sugar is completely dissolved. Simmer the fig jam over moderate heat, stirring occasionally, until the fruit is soft and the liquid runs off the side of a spoon in thick, heavy drops.

Remove from heat and spoon into jam jars, close and process the jars (boiling the closed jar and its contents for at least 10 minutes.

Doce de melão (Melon jam)

In some summers there were so many melons that my Aunts had to be prepare them into jam because they could not eat so many melons!

1 melon
Juice of 1 lemon
The equal weight of the melon in sugar

Cut melon into slices and remove seeds and skin (try not to cut too close to the skin as the flesh near here remains quite hard and crunchy). Cube melon flesh and

combine with sugar and lemon in a bowl. Let macerate overnight.
Pour the melon and all its juices into a large heavy-bottomed pan. Bring to a rapid boil and cook, on high heat, for about 25 minutes or until the jam is set. During this time, stir it often.
Remove from heat and spoon into jam jars, close and process the jars (boiling the closed jar and its contents for at least 10 minutes).

Doce de tomate (Tomato jam)

In the summer it rains tomatoes in Alentejo. As there were no fridges, my Aunts used to make tomato jam.

1 kg tomato, peeled, cored, and coarsely chopped
1 kg sugar
Juice of 1 lemon

Add all the ingredients to a heavy bottom saucepan and bring the mixture to a boil, stirring frequently to prevent the bottom from burning.
Reduce the heat and simmer, stirring occasionally, until the mixture has thickened to the consistency of jam.
Remove from heat and spoon into jam jars, close and process the jars (boiling the closed jar and its contents for at least 10 minutes).

Geleia de marmelo (Quince jelly)

The Aunts used to make the quince jelly at the same time as they did the quince jam.

Quince skin and seeds
Sugar

Put quince skin and seeds in a large stockpot with a thick bottom and add enough water to cover all pieces. Bring to a boil, reduce heat to simmer, cover, and cook for 45 minutes to an hour.
Strain the liquid. Measure the amount of juice you have. For each litre of liquid, add 1kg of sugar. Pour strained quince juice into a thick-bottomed pot on the stove and bring to a boil. Add sugar to the juice.
Bring to a boil, initially stirring constantly, until the sugar is dissolved, so that the sugar does not stick to the bottom of the pan. As the jelly cooks, skim off the foam that comes to the surface with a spoon.
To know if the jelly is ready, you do the test. Put a half teaspoonful of the jelly on a chilled (in the freezer) plate. Allow the jelly to cool a few seconds, then push it with your fingertip. If it wrinkles up, it's ready.
Remove from the heat and spoon into jam jars, close and process the jars (boiling the closed jar and its contents for at least 10 minutes).

Marmelada (Red quince jam)

Letter from Zé to his sisters Cecília and Maria, 16.10.1968: "Do not peel the quince, it is cut in four parts. Remove the seeds and the rotten parts, wash them and bring them to boil, until they are cooked. You have to beat the quince mash, as if it were a cake,. While you are beating add the sugar, always beating. This paste is then put back in the pan, boiled for 10 minutes, and removed from the heat. Divide the paste into bowls, cover with baking paper. You do not have to put it in the sun to dry."

1 kg quince, washed, stems removed, cored, quartered
1 kg sugar

Put quince pieces in a large stockpot with a thick bottom and add enough water to cover the pieces of quince. Bring to a boil, reduce heat to simmer, cover and cook for 45 minutes to an hour, until the quince pieces are soft.
Mash the quince. Add sugar, beating constantly,
Bring to the boil. Lower the heat and let it simmer for 10 minutes, stirring constantly. Put into bowls and leave to cool. Cover with baking paper.

Marmelada clara (White quince jam)

This white quince jam is made with unripe gamboas. *Those are bigger than quinces, less acidic, and sweeter.*

1 kg de *gamboas* (a type of quince)
800 g sugar

In a large sauce pan place the whole quinces. Add cold water to cover and bring to a boil. Reduce heat, cover the pan and simmer until tender, about 30-40 minutes. Drain contents of the pan into a colander. Remove skin and seeds. Using a blender or a food processor puree quince into a homogenous pulp, in batches if necessary. Place puree into a large saucepan and heat to medium-low, then stir in sugar. Continue to heat, stirring constantly, until sugar dissolves.
Cook over low heat, uncovered, stirring occasionally, until puree is very thick. If you have a syrup-weigher, it should be 37° Baumé (or 115°C on a thermometer).

Playing farmer (1972)

Other recipes

Arroz de feijão verde (Green beans rice)

My Aunt used to sow greens beans every year.

1 dl olive oil
300 g green beans, ends trimmed off and cut into rhombuses
1 onion, peeled and chopped
1 garlic clove, peeled and chopped
Chopped parsley
Salt
2 cups rice
4 cups boiling water

Heat olive oil in a pan over medium heat and saute green beans, onion, garlic, and parsley.
Add rice, salt, and boiling water. Cover pan, lower the heat and cook for 10 -15 minutes.

Feijão verde com ovos (Green beans with eggs)

In summer there are green beans every where.

Green beans, ends trimmed off and cut into rhombuses
Salt
1 onion, peeled and chopped
1 clove garlic, peeled and chopped
1 tablespoon lard
4 eggs, beaten
Butter
A few drops of lemon juice
Pepper

Place green beans and salt in a pan, cover with boiling water and cook them until *al dente*.
Remove and drain.
In a sauce pan, sauté onion and garlic in lard.
When the onion is translucent, add cooked green beans.
Mix well.

Add beaten eggs. Keep temperature low and keep stiring when cooking the eggs so the bottom doesn't get too brown or overcooked.
Add butter, lemon juice, and a little pepper. Mix well.
Serve with slices of fried bread.

In the estate with Lena (1972)

Massa de pimentão (Red bell pepper paste)

This paste is a popular seasoning in Alentejo.

When the red bell peppers are ripe and very red, open them vertically and seed them. Wash them.
Cut them into strips. Place the strips in a clay pot in alternate layers with coarse salt.
Leave them for at least 30 days (max 90 days). This operation is called "tanning".
After this time, drain, wash and pat dry the pepper strips.
Mince them. Put the paste in jam jars, cover the surface with 1.5 cm of olive oil. As you use the paste, do not forget to keep the surface of the paste with olive oil to prevent mould developing.

Pãezinhos de torresmos (Cracklings rolls)

Cracklings, or scratchings, are the solid material which remains after rendering pork fat and skin. It is often eaten as a snack food, but also used in cooking.

25 g fresh yeast
3 tablespoons sugar
1 tablespoon salt
3 cups warm water
½ cup lard
6 cups all purpose flour
450 g cracklings

In a bowl, crumble fresh yeast into some water and some sugar, and stir until dissolved. Place flour in a large bowl and make a well in the middle. Give the yeast mixture to the flour, add water and lard, and mix well. Knead well using the kneading attachments of your mixer or with your hands, until it no longer sticks in your hands. Add half the quantity of crackling and knead the dough well. Cover with a clean kitchen cloth and let the dough rise in a warm place. It should double in size. Preheat oven to 200° C. Take the dough out of the bowl, shape 3 round rolls and place them on a tray dusted with flour. Let rise again for about 20 minutes. Sprinkle the remaining cracklings on top and bake in the preheated oven for 30 minutes.

Pão alentejano (Alentejo bread)

Alentejo bread is known for its characteristic tangy flavour, chewy texture and crisp, crackly crust. When you bake for the 1st time, you'll have to prepare your own sourdough starter. For future breads, take little piece of the leavened dough and keep it in the fridge until you bake a new bread.

For the sourdough starter:
200 g rye flour
2 tablespoons buttermilk
250 ml water

For the bread:
50 g fresh yeast
1 teaspoon sugar
400 ml sourdough starter
1 kg all purpose flour
2 tablespoons salt
1 cup lukewarm water

The sourdough starter takes 5 days to prepare. On day 1, put in a jar 100 g rye flour, pour in 125 ml lukewarm water and buttermilk. Whisk well with a fork until it's lump-free. Then, let it rest at room temperature until it becomes bubbly and active. On day 2 and 3, just whisk the mixture with a fork. On day 4, add 125 ml lukewarm water and 100 g rye flour. Whisk well and let it rest at

room temperature. On day 5, your starter is ready to use. For the bread, crumble fresh yeast into some water and sugar and stir until dissolved. Let rest for 10 minutes. Place flour in a large bowl and make a well in the middle. Give the yeast mixture to the flour, add the rest of the ingredients, and mix well. Knead well using the kneading attachments of your mixer or with your hands. Cover with a clean kitchen cloth and let the dough rise in a warm place for 2 hours. It should double in size.
Take the dough out of the bowl, shape 1 or 2 round breads (don't forget the "head" of the Alentejo bread) and place them on a tray dusted with flour. Do not place them too close together as they will rise. Cover the cakes with a cloth and let them rise again for 20 minutes.
Preheat oven to 225 °C. On the bottom of the oven put a baking tray with boiling water.
Bake for 10 minutes, Lower the heat to 200 °C and bake for further 40 – 50 minutes.

Bibliography

MAIA, Carlos Bento (1904 / 1995), Tratado completo de cozinha e de copa. Lisboa, Publicações Dom Quixote

MOTA, Maria Vicência Baptista (1999), *Enchidos de Cabeço de Vide.* Portalegre, Ed. João Ribeirinho Leal

PEREIRA-MÜLLER, M. Margarida (1995), *Variações em pão.* Mem Martins, Publicações Europa-América

RIGAUD, Lucas (1807), *O Cozinheiro Moderno ou Nova Arte de Cozinha.* Lisboa, Typografia Lacerda

Rua de Avis

Contents

My Aunts Maria and Cecília with their grandnieces (1986)

Printed by Amazon Italia Logistica S.r.l.
Torrazza Piemonte (TO), Italy

43694861R00093